T0195019

REINVENTING LIFE

My Journey into PTSD and Back

ILMARINEN VOGEL

BALBOA.PRESS

A DIVISION OF HAY HOUSE

Balboa Press books may be ordered through booksellers or by contacting:

Balboa Press
A Division of Hay House
1663 Liberty Drive
Bloomington, IN 47403
www.balboapress.com
1 (877) 407-4847

Because of the dynamic nature of the Internet, any web addresses or links contained in this book may have changed since publication and may no longer be valid. The views expressed in this work are solely those of the author and do not necessarily reflect the views of the publisher, and the publisher hereby disclaims any responsibility for them.

The author of this book does not dispense medical advice or prescribe the use of any technique as a form of treatment for physical, emotional, or medical problems without the advice of a physician, either directly or indirectly. The intent of the author is only to offer information of a general nature to help you in your quest for emotional and spiritual well-being. In the event you use any of the information in this book for yourself, which is your constitutional right, the author and the publisher assume no responsibility for your actions.

Any people depicted in stock imagery provided by Getty Images are models, and such images are being used for illustrative purposes only. Certain stock imagery © Getty Images.

Print information available on the last page.

ISBN: 978-1-9822-3868-1 (sc)
ISBN: 978-1-9822-3870-4 (hc)
ISBN: 978-1-9822-3869-8 (e)

Balboa Press rev. date: 11/15/2019

CHAPTER ONE

INTRODUCTION

There are two parts to my story. One describes my journey that leads from a small village in post war Europe to places that became dear to me and to people who taught me about themselves by letting me observe them. I will describe places I discovered and people I encountered along the way. To protect the identity of individuals all names of persons and the actual places have been changed or omitted.

This journey will be presented as a memoir. It contains scenes I remember and stories I was told by friends and family. The desire to write my story emerged after I was injured in a head on collision with an impact speed of 120 mph New Year's Eve of 2008. A seventeen-year-old child was in the vehicle with me. We were struck by an oncoming vehicle in a blind curve in our lane. There was no time to react. This accident ended my life and my world as I knew it. It put me into a place I didn't know existed. It forced me down to the bottom of a black hole. I had to learn how to climb out and find the light again, once I had reached rock bottom. The alternative would have been to end my own life. In the process of learning how to reconnect with my life I realized how many people there are, who have suffered trauma. I learned that there is a hidden side to trauma that no one can see. It is more difficult to treat and takes longer to heal than the physical wounds we can watch as they heal. Trauma victims are in need of protection, encouragement, counselling and therapy without drugs, long after the physical wounds are healed. It is impossible to see the shift in the mind of an injured person that takes them from functioning well, to being disconnected, paranoid and one inch away from homelessness and suicide. The victim still looks the same as she or he did the day before the trauma happened. This book is more about trauma than about myself. I am just one of the victims and my recovery is one of many.

I recognize those who stood by me even though I was unable to see them, hear them or to show them my appreciation. Outstanding was the encouragement and help I received from my trauma counsellor who stopped the race to ending my life. I reached a point in my healing process at which confronting my past was holding the key to full recovery. Understanding and forgiving myself and others, took a great burden off my shoulders. I share these experiences, hoping that it might help my readers find their own healing process and to bring hope to those who feel embarrassed or ashamed by a condition, that they have fallen victim to, without fault of their own.

May you seek help. It can be done. You are not alone.

I am sorry, please forgive me. I thank you and I love you.

CHAPTER TWO

BEGINNING

I was born into the chaos of the years following World War Two. Millions of people were waiting to settle into their lives, trying to find work or housing, moving from temporary to permanent shelter in a world that had to be reinvented and reconstructed. My parents, who had been openly opposed to the National Socialist party, had barely escaped with their lives. They had only a very small chance of surviving the Nazi regime in Germany. They abandoned the plans for their own lives. My mother would have liked to study medicine and my father was fascinated with art history and archeology. My mother became pregnant, which exempted her from having to manufacture bullets for Hitler's war. My father studied medicine and joined the medical corps, saving lives as a physician, rather than taking lives as a soldier.

My parents had made a vow to one another, not to abandon the fight for social, economic or environmental justice and to stand for freedom of choice, freedom of science, medicine, education and human rights. This included a vow not to leave their homeland, but to start a family and to outlast the threat. Temporary housing and frequent moves were a fate they shared with millions of refugees and late returnees from prisons of war abroad. All were perceived as a threat to local residents who were lucky enough to still live in their inherited homes and environment. Lack of available housing caused their forced separation, lasting almost ten years. Work and housing were not yet available at the same location. This shaped the relationships with our father, our mother and my siblings.

I grew up in the shadow of two world wars, surrounded by traumatized people who had seen their world upended and completely changed several times in less than fifty Years. The loss of family members and entire parts of society and the trauma of forced relocation was slowly entering the collective conscience and psyche. Mourning was setting in as shock wore off and the glory of heroic war tales began to lose their luster. My parents were both children of ministers, who were struggling with the fact that their religion did not provide answers to the question:

"Why is it necessary to destroy creation in the name of the creator or of dictators who coronate themselves as a divine right and arm their subjects against one another to threaten dissenters, who are asking questions or demand a piece of the pie?

Why was there nothing in religious culture that could prevent this tragedy of the loss and displacement of millions of lives around the world?"

In their search for answers, my parents and their parents before them were tirelessly studying ancient religions and indigenous cultures, to see if they could detect a place in time where mankind lost its path to an ordained life, or at least to peaceful coexistence and non violent conflict resolution. They found no quick answers, but had to settle for learning how to ask better questions. Being the next generation and listening to our grownups talk and agonize over these questions during meals, I began feeling subordinated to this quest for freedom and justice. I was just a kid. There were meals with father presiding. I was not asked about my opinion. It was different while I was in the sole care of my mother. I was told stories from mythology and sagas, Nordic Buddhist Vedic Greek Roman Germanic Celtic and Bask. Some of the stories, my parents had collected personally from oral accounts in northern and eastern Europe. While spinning and weaving, my mother told countless fairy tales at bedtime. She read to me the writings from the court of King Arthur and the poetry of travelling minstrels. That was the world she had created for me and herself.

Recently, I read my parent's almost daily correspondence from the Years during the War and during their separation after the war. I learned that they were expecting new ideas and impulses to be delivered to them by their children as we had just arrived from the Spirit World. They referred to us as "messengers". Did they listen to us? What was the message we brought? Would anyone remember to ask? I remember this much: Society and Religious leaders were fresh out of ideas what to do or say, since everything they knew from their bible studies had now failed them three times in one lifetime. One day in reflecting my parent's prayers it occurred to me that I had indeed brought something into my family's life, that was stronger than the ebbs and storms, successes and failures of daily life: Unconditional love and unbreakable loyalty.

My gratitude goes to people I was privileged to encounter, to learn from, to choose as guides and mentors and to give me inspiration. Each challenging me to qualify myself for the task at hand and to learn from the language, expression and example of their lives. I looked at what people do. I listened to their opinions but found that they changed, depending on whom they were talking to.

My journey will include my confrontation with Post Traumatic Stress Disorder, which is afflicting several generations of people from around the world. My discovery was that it is a disorder that can be healed without drugs.

After my return from living and working for six Years in New York City to New England I once again engaged in building custom homes for discerning clients. I was privileged to work with talented craftsmen in the most beautiful locations on this spectacular coast. A new network of craftsmen and vendors had to be established. I visited a fellow builder, who was showing me a post and beam house he had constructed for his family. During this tour my host explained that it was due to therapy for Post-Traumatic Stress Disorder provided by the U.S. Veterans Administration that he had regained his ability to live a productive life and to start a new family. He told me that he had suffered a complete breakdown, resulting in the loss of his first family after returning from a foreign War with episodes of depression and domestic violence and a total inability to communicate with his loved ones. He spoke about violence towards his wife and children which prompted the courts to ban all contact with a restraining order.

"Would You tell me more about this, when we have time?" I asked.

"Absolutely, I will be glad to" he replied.

We met for coffee. After more than two hours he had finished his story. I told him:

"You know what you have just done? You have told me the story of my life with my own father. You have told me what happened to him and what had happened to me. By sharing your story with me, you have given me a chance to begin a new search for answers. I might have a chance to heal. I will be forever grateful for your generosity. You have also told me the story about several friends of mine who have struggled with PTSD with tragic and often lethal outcomes. I will walk through life with an open eye for this condition as I find it. I will be grateful to you for opening to me this window into your successful recovery and for providing me with a mirror in which I can see myself in the future."

I realized how little we all know about this and how hard it is to relate to an illness, that shows no visible scars and has as many faces as it has victims. I resolved to learn more about PTSD. I began to pay attention to domestic violence. I was told that often there is no recollection of violent episodes in people who suffer from PTSD. I noticed in my own recollections and in the accounts of others the complete absence of hate or fear towards persons who commit acts of violence during episodes caused by PTSD. When I was five years old, I remember thinking that there was something in my father's persona that caused such episodes of violence towards me and that he was not quite himself while they lasted.

I resolved for myself, that I would never touch another human being if at all possible. I became a conscientious objector. I never considered violence to be an option in resolving conflict. I took training in alternative dispute resolution. As a volunteer community mediator I served to help resolve conflicts between parties outside of the courtroom, giving people a chance to participate in crafting acceptable settlements and good agreements. To further my mediation skills I participated in a "Project on Negotiation". This experience was later helpful when I headed a home restoration service. Managing customer relations and their expectations as well as facilitating manager's meetings, leading multiple projects requiring collaboration, skill and information sharing by participating workmen and clients benefitted from this training.

The next chapter will lead into my own descend into Post- Traumatic Stress Disorder. This was accompanied by a stream of memories rushing in from my past.

CHAPTER THREE

DRIVE INTO A NEW WORLD

It Is New Year's Eve. We are going to celebrate with friends. The evening is chilly, no moisture in the air, no wind, no ice on the road. The light is dimming, creating the steel blue skies of New England winters. The silhouette of bushes and trees is in stark contrast, black against steel blue skies. As we round a rock outcropping to descend towards the lake the gentle curve of the road and the curve of the shoreline appear to be merging creating perfect intersecting lines matched only by the soft harmony of nostalgic love songs on our car radio. We are feeling good. We are looking forward to a New Year's Eve celebration in the company of dear friends. The mirror smooth surface of the lake is reflecting distant hills upside down with sharp outlines of the horizon backlit by the afterglow of the setting sun in stunning clarity. The water seems to retain extra light making reflections appear brighter than the sky. We are talking about tonight's New Years Eve party with friends. My seventeen-year old passenger is about to say:

BAM. SSSSSSSS

Acrid smell of gunpowder,
battery acid, gasoline, oil and cooling liquid
are filling the air.
The boom of the impact an elongated crunch.
Our windshield shatters in an explosion
our airbags deploy.

Suddenly it is completely quiet. Just the hissing.
It is almost dark outside.
I hear breathing next to me.
In the rear-view mirror, I can see the lights of cars stopped behind me.
How long has it been?

I am tapping forward to find the warning light switch.
Nothing. It does not work.

My brain is roaming.
Where am I?
What just happened?

I remember that in the split second before impact
I had formulated a single thought.
I am going to have to let this happen!
A large white truck appeared sideways
in the low beam of my vehicle
in my lane, no headlights visible.
It is gone.

It is now quiet. Just the hissing.
My ears are ringing in a high pitch
somewhere towards the center of my skull.

I am numb
Only the hissing sound

I hear breathing
I hear moaning
My passenger

Oh my God
I forgot about my passenger.
How long has it been?
I am disoriented
I have trouble breathing
I cannot remember.

My passenger.
Oh my God
The smell
The explosion in my face
The smell of gunpowder
steam and smoke
the windshield gone
shards of glass in my mouth
I think I broke a molar

I hear breathing
I hear moaning
focus, damn it get her out!
I have to get her out,
this could blow any second.

Brain now in overdrive
I am going into a state
I can focus.
I have one thought:
Get her out!

Seatbelts,
my clip,

her clip,
her door.

I run around the car,
get her out now!
my brain repeats
now!
I get to her door,
try to open it.
It does not open.
shit, shit, shit!

Explosive smell.
Go.
Around the car again.
Inside over my seat
I grab her shoulders
I pull her up
I see blood

I move her
she is helping
fighting
kicking
across the shifter
across my seat
head under door frame.

I lift her up
legs under her
she faints
I turn her around.
I hold her from behind
We move away from the wreck.

Ilmarinen Vogel

The smell,
the steam,
the hissing.
Out of reach of fire.
Out of reach of explosion.

Leaning on a guard rail.
Breathing,
headlights through steam,
we are not alone.
An urgent voice
speaking on a cell phone:
"Police…. yes
we need everything
below the Uptown Inn.

Yes ambulances...
blind curve...
traffic control
please
now
thank you.

It is not as dark anymore
headlights behind
headlights ahead
emergency blinkers
leaning against the guard rail
holding my passenger from behind
trying to keep her warm
someone hands me blankets
to wrap her in.
Given by friends,
who are living across the street
from the accident.

They heard the crash
they rushed to help.
My brain is trying to process...
a ghost truck appeared,
disappeared on impact.
All went dark.
I could not see it coming.
Now I am breathing shallow breaths.
Something is wrong with my chest.
the body of my passenger in my arms.
Still limp,
wrapped in blankets,
breathing.
Unconscious.

I know the person driving the car behind us.
She called for help.
I know the people in the house across the street.
They brought the blankets.
The ambulance arrives.

I know the first responder.
We both volunteer with the National Ski Patrol.
I know the Fire Chief.
We serve on Committees together.
I know the police officers.
I repaired the station house.
I am surrounded by friends.
I know everyone.

My passenger is regaining consciousness.
We move her into the warmth of the fire chief's truck
I listen to the emergency channel.
"You want me to order pizza?"
I ask.

Chuckles.
Good.
Humor is back.

Roadblocks being set,
detours arranged,
ambulances dispatched.
I am feeling grateful for first responders.

Lucky about the comfort of community.
It is New Year's Eve 2008.
"Take us to a hospital
close to home.

New Years Eve Party
at the Emergency room."
Another chuckle.
We are alive
we arrive,
skeleton staff.

X-rays sent to Pennsylvania,
my rib cage is broken,
nothing to be done,
still in shock.

Stitches on my passenger's forehead.
Airbag slammed her right wrist
into her left eyebrow.
Wrist needs examination,
friction heat of seatbelt
caused burn across chest.
Through cotton shirt,
trough sweatshirt,
through down jacket.

Vitals taken,
bandages applied,
pain meds given,
I am besides myself
I am acting brave.

Home by three thirty 2009,
we can walk,
both in shock,
feeling nothing.

Now looking for the world
from the evening before.
It is gone.
Now is 2009.

Chapter Four

SLIPPING

Ankles, shins, knees, hips, shoulders, neck, wrists, left hand and lower back swollen and stiff all hiding behind chest pain. The tiniest movement is excruciating. It radiates from my chest. Shock is wearing off. Adrenaline has drained away. Pain is driving tears into eyes. I am breathing tiny shallow breaths. My rib cage is screaming.

"You have a fracture near your solar plexus where the seat belt caught your chest. Nothing we can do. Let it heal by itself. We can give you pain meds. This prescription you can pick up at the pharmacy."

Sleep seems to be interrupted once every hour. I know there is more wrong with me than my ribcage. Forty-five minutes to plan how to get out of bed. No leverage on any part of my body. Slip over the side of the bed to the floor. Try to get a leg under me. Put pressure on my knees. Fifteen minutes to reach the bathroom. Only half awake the sensation is that of a heart attack. Chest pain left shoulder, left wrist and pain down the left arm. Shortness of breath. Half asleep I go for aspirin and water.

Then I wake up. Now I remember the accident. I am in need of medical attention. My mobility is gone. New places around my body begin swelling. Left wrist and every bone in my left hand are severely bruised. No mobility in my left shoulder. Knees, shins and ankles bruised. Pain is beginning to spike through my chest pain in ever new places.

"Bone bruises are the worst and take the longest to heal." I am told. Muscles cramping at night.

"Take some Calcium and Magnesium" Someone suggests.

"No one is experienced with head on collisions. People usually don't survive. Did you see your car? Oh my God. Do you have any idea how lucky you are?"

I begin to resent sentences that start with "you just" or "all you have to" or "don't even try". Meanwhile at night my muscles are a concert of cramps that are talking to one another from side to side checkmating me for an hour until I finally find a way to release them one at a time. Breathing out helps. Once I am standing up, I can let the calf muscles stretch and relax. Pain of cramps is no longer covered by chest pain. Charley horse some are calling it. Toe cramps are most wicked.

Sleep deprivation is slowly and imperceptibly turning my brain to a state of ever deepening fatigue. I cannot explain this to anyone. I still look the same as I did just a few days ago. A little bent over. I am beginning to enter a mental zombie state. Waking up every hour is beginning to cause memory malfunction. Luckily, I am in the habit of writing everything down. Home repairs. Myriads of details.

One morning I am going to the pharmacy for a prescription. At an intersection I am waiting for the light to turn green. I wake up when a car behind me sounds its horn. I had just travelled sixty miles at a speed of seventy-five mph. Falling asleep could have happened while I was driving. I immediately went to the hospital and signed myself into a sleep lab for an overnight test. This was more than not normal.

During the sleep test the attendant attached wires to all parts of my head and chest. There was a window through which I was being observed. I tried to fall asleep with deep exhalations and finally succeeded after I had accepted the fact that I was completely entangled in wires. I was diagnosed with Sleep Apnea. I learned that my sleep was not interrupted once every hour as I had observed, but once every two and a half minutes. The doctor said:

"This sleep pattern never lets you reach REM sleep. It will prevent your healing process." This accounted for my deep fatigue. It explained why all my symptoms from the crash were getting worse as time went on.

"We will give you supplemental oxygen." The doctor said. I was fitted with a bi pap machine, which adds oxygen to the air I breathe. I had to wear an apparatus during the night, making my breathing sound like Darth Vader. I was now being continuously monitored with a recording device I was wearing on my chest and wrist. It recorded my heartbeat and my breathing. The doctors off- loaded this information every two weeks.

At home I was beginning to feel static caused by resentment about "one thing after another", which set in motion a whole new level of stress. I felt guilty and embarrassment was felt by everyone, when I fell asleep during concerts or during school theater productions when suddenly a loud snoring breath escaped me, which of course I did not hear unless it was so loud that it woke me up. Trying to get my life back, including trying to do my chores around the house. It was a priority for me. Only now everything took three times as long. No one seemed to find anything wrong with me, except that I was acting strange and selfish.

I continued going to work, where my great team members were doing all they could to help me out. Especially with range of motion issues such as climbing into tight spaces to inspect buildings. They did it for me and reported what they had found. I then made programs for repairs and wrote estimates and work orders. Every activity was exhausting. I needed to take an extended midday-break at home to get lunch and to rest. Bathroom breaks included getting into the shower to wash up. This added two hours to my work day. I insisted on getting everything done, to deliver to my clients the service they had come to expect.

I came home every day completely spent, unable to interact with my family. Like a vegetable I was parked in front of the TV not even flipping through channels. I was sinking deeper and deeper inside myself. I was unaware that I was just about mute. I could not talk on the outside. Could not reach out. I was all alone and deep inside.

To understand the legal side of my condition, I retained a lawyer to deal with the accident. On his advice, I engaged a second lawyer. A workman's compensation specialist. To help me with workman's compensation insurance issues. This accident was work-related. A job inspection put me into harm's way at this location at this time. Therefore, my medical needs and loss of income were supposed to be covered by Workman's Compensation Insurance as required by State Law. It took fourteen months to win approval of my workmen's compensation claim. To make things worse, I had to sue my employer, to be able to force my insurance claim against Workman's Comp.

During this time I was continuously working, while trying to treat my injuries with only my personal health insurance. I realized that my insurance was failing me when my doctors were limiting treatment to what my insurance would cover. Not to what my medical needs were to heal my injuries. This was a betrayal.

Up to now, everything had come out of my own pocket, because insurance for my family and myself was available only after an eight-thousand-dollar deductible. In addition to this, I had to come up with enormous co-payments, once the insurance did cover something. I discovered that I had been sold an insufficient safety net, which added another layer to my stress. I was running out of money. Friends began sending me rescue checks to prevent a default on my mortgage. Without their help I would have lost my home.

Another shock was, that after being severely injured at work, compensation insurance dropped sick leave pay to sixty five percent of regular wages. That coincided with my new skyrocketing expenses. This was another betrayal, weighing heavily on my mind. I now was not only worried about losing my home, I was making my wife upset and going into debt. I was also worried about being disabled to the point of defaulting on my job. This was before the insurance finally agreed to pay for several operations. Each request was first answered with a resounding "no". There were going to be rehabilitation periods of nine months after every operation. We were just beginning to develop a plan. Still more MRIs and CT scans. Like a brewing hurricane a feeling of doom began coming over me. Pain was still getting worse. I was depending on my family doctor for help. In August (eight months after the accident) he sent me back to my orthopedic surgeon. Images taken after the accident were now re-examined. After initially analyzing the MRIs in January the surgeons had sent me to physical therapy for shoulder, hip, knee, neck and lower back issues. Aquatic exercise and gentle tugging on my limbs had been prescribed. Also, some "Stim" a vibrator with jelly used here and there. Now inflammation and joint pain in all my joints and in my left shoulder began to be intolerable. I was in rapid decline and within a few months I felt as though I had aged two or three decades. Walking with bent knees hurt my knees as I was trying to protect them, while my physicians now told me that I had age related arthritis.

The week before the accident, I was out in the Hills, doing hard, fast trekking training with my partner for a trip to Machu Picchu in Peru. No age-related arthritis there. I now came to the conclusion that this accident had disabled me permanently.

"You cannot fix your shoulder with physical therapy," my orthopedic surgeon told me. "You need an operation. Your rotator cuff is torn."

"I cannot fix my shoulder? Last time I checked, you were the doctor and I the patient. Everything your office told me to do, I did. Now it is eight months after the accident and you are telling me I cannot fix my shoulder with Physical Therapy and that I need an operation?"

"Yes." The surgeon replied.

"I am about to explode" I squeezed these words between my clenched teeth. "I will remove myself from your office and slowly walk out of this room. After I close this door, I will never set foot in this office again. I will find a real surgeon and have my shoulder and whatever else you did not find repaired by a real professional." I was on fire and deeply distressed.

The search for a qualified surgeon and a physical therapist took eleven months and an operation on my shoulder was planned for the following July. Nineteen Months of extreme suffering, nine months of physical therapy, during which I was now officially on sick leave, followed by knee surgery. Nine more months of physical therapy before I was able to return to work. Once back at the office I was told that I had to be laid off for lack of work. To save my house I applied for disability retirement and was immediately granted early full retirement. My battle with the insurance companies and accident liability claims were going on with no end in sight. This took out all the fight I had left in me. Everyone was furious about my decision to file for early disability retirement. The man who drove into the accident had disappeared. Full recovery from this accident will not be possible. To function reasonably well took ten years.

Following is the story of my struggle with my mental injuries, which were far worse and harder to treat than the physical ones. This would lead me into territory unknown to me. Unknown to anyone I know, including my physician. I lost everything I held dear, except for my life and that had to be reinvented if I were to be able to continue living.

Chapter Five

SUICIDE

One day while driving to a client's property for an inspection tears began running down my cheeks. The stream was so strong that I had to pull off the road because I was unable to see. I was feeling overwhelming grief. This was shocking the first time it happened. It happened again and began happening with greater frequency during a period of just a few weeks. Shortly after this flooding started, I found myself looking for ways to end my life. My mind was having its own conversations. I began thinking that I was the cause of all the problems for my company, my community and my family. The economy was stalling. My health was getting worse rather than better and I felt useless.

My brain began to reason that finishing myself off would solve all problems. The mortgage and many new expenses would be paid for by the payout from my life insurance. There would have to be another accident. I was unable to talk to anyone about this. Screams on the inside became louder. The silence was deafening. Like a drowning person I was not screaming or flailing my arms. Instead I was watching myself quietly sink. Without directing my thoughts and feelings, I began experiencing and reliving everything that ever happened to me in my life: Injuries, betrayals, disappointments, heartbreaks and losses. Everything suddenly appeared through a filter of pain.

Finally I projected the end of my family and my marriage. I felt like the world was falling on my head. One by one in random order incessantly and inescapably, emotions began to wash over me. Physical injuries appeared to be healing, leaving just a few little scars that would eventually disappear. With an outwardly stoic, positive attitude and my workouts in the pool I seemed to be on the mend. Part of me thought I was ok, another part of me became more concerned. Every white truck that came into my field of vision caused me to react strongly. It broke my heart.

My greatest pain was not the result of my physical injuries: It was my inability to forgive myself. I was unable to cope with this. I kept punishing myself for driving into this crash. I caught myself looking for a way and a place to finish the job the white truck had started.

I realized that I had become suicidal. I began fighting for my life. I knew I needed help. Physically I was not getting better, I was slipping ever so imperceptibly, as my fatigue was deepening and my mobility was fading. I did not use the term "disabled" in my mind. The indignity of my condition and the feeling of being alone right in the middle of my family, friends and loved ones, my crew, my company, my community began to bear heavy on my heart. I had no language and no name for this feeling. Nothing had prepared me for this. I was living in an environment that I had grown to love. Suddenly my entire life began to fall on top of me.

The combination of having no language to explain what I was feeling and everyone around me still seeing the person from a few days, weeks and months ago, unable to fathom the change that had taken place inside of me, isolated me. One day, without warning, I began to cry. Tears were flooding. I had to pull over. The sense of being completely alone was washing over me with every new wave of tears. My life was suddenly racing before my mind's eye in five-year increments in fast forward. Each of these memories was causing a new wave of flooding. I was watching the chapters of a story, which I was intimately familiar with. I could not stop it from playing. Trapped in these emotional memories, I was experiencing a feeling of complete failure. Only heartbreak made it through the filter of my broken mind. Pain was now attaching itself to every scene, as it had become my constant companion since the accident. Heartbreak was the theme of my memory in my deep fatigue. I needed to do something:

I thought of two things to do:

First, I was invited to participate as pit man on a racing boat during a New England Race week. The pit man is the person who raises and drops sails standing below in the boat. A position I had held in the past. Adrenalin would help me do this job despite my pain. I was hoping this would reconnect me with my life and I was grateful for such an opportunity.

Second, I went to see my doctor about my suicidal thoughts. The doctor said:

"I have something for you, that will make you feel better".

When I came home that night, I read the label and the fine print. It said: Warning. Side effect: May cause suicide. I was livid.

"You don't have an appointment," said the receptionist at my doctor's office when I stormed in the next day.

"Yes, I do. I have an appointment with my life. The doctor gave me a prescription against suicide. One of the side effect of this drug is suicide." She let me in to see the doctor.

"I need you to refer me to a therapist who does not use drugs that might kill me. I have never disobeyed doctor's orders before. This time I do. I am not ready to become a victim to a drug." The doctor named a therapist. The name of the counsellor was familiar to me. I had done work on his house. He knew how I worked and how I functioned. We liked and respected each other. I went to see him. After telling him the reason I had been sent, we spoke for the length of a session and he set up the next appointment. I felt that I was in good hands now. During the next session, he said:

"You have all the symptoms of Post-Traumatic Stress Disorder. Not only did you get traumatized by this accident but you were traumatized before. I see big T's and little T's in your history. I do not believe in making you relive past trauma or to re-traumatize my patients. Instead we will look at each item as it comes up in your mind. Meanwhile, we will work on building coping skills and setting the stage for healing. I am a veteran from the Vietnam war. I was traumatized there and learned about the possibility of healing PTSD. I became a counsellor. I now work with Veterans traumatized by war. For a number of Years, I have worked with the Wounded Warriors Project. We do individual counselling and also bring entire families for long weekend conferences. Engaging families is important because on their own they have no way to look inside of their injured loved ones. It is impossible for them to understand what is happening to them and to their children. Together we build coping skills for entire families".

"Should I bring my wife and my daughter to our sessions?"

"Why don't we work on your trauma until we know more. Then we make this call." He suggested. "Let's get out of suicide watch first. Tell me more about the flooding. Flooding is very common in PTSD sufferers".

I explained:

"Recently floods of memories and a stream of tears happen simultaneously. Suddenly there it is. Once it starts, it is impossible to stop it. I now have a filter in my mind that alters what I see. It presents everything I remember as a failure. In the past I was able to recognize and manage pain or to ignore it. I have never felt pain with such intensity as I do now while memories are coming up. Both physically and emotionally. I feel pain now that in the past I was able to ignore and to block."

"Why don't you tell me about the memories that hurt you, worry you. Even the ones that scare you. Speaking about them might help us to reset them," the counselor said. "Tell me where you came from. My family is from Europe. I am sure we have a lot of cultural background in common." Now he was ready to listen.

I explained the moments of flooding in my car that were accompanied with floods of memories in which everything that I remembered was suddenly the story of failure after failure.

CHAPTER SIX

THE FOOTHILLS

"I see myself in early childhood roaming the foothills of the Alps. I see the stunningly beautiful vistas of big sky merged into snow-capped mountain tops supported by steep rock faces framed by rubble fields, streams, waterfalls and vegetation from small alpine flowers and grasses to flowering bushes and trees. I see colors white, sky blue royal blue, dusty gray haze to green and black shadows in folds and alpine valleys.

Suddenly I am torn from this world in which I was free to roam, using deer trails and brooks as my guides. Never did I get lost and always did I find my way home. I am forced to move to a world that is not safe for me only to be closer to my father. Closer, but not with him. Even though I am looking forward to the adventure of finally getting on that train that had taken him away from us time and time again after his visits, only to leave us in tears seconds after he had waved goodbye and disappeared with the train down the track. I was two years old at the time."

"How did you get there?" The therapist asked.

I was now completely overwhelmed with grief
over the loss of my world at that time.

"I was born two days before Christmas on my oldest brother's third birthday. I was the result of a celebration of life, of two young people surviving the Second World War. My parents celebrated their reunion and the end of the Nazi Era after several years of separation. My father had served as a surgeon and succeeded to walk out of the POW internment camp to find my mother and my two older siblings in the Alps, where she had found refuge. My parent's survival was somewhat of a miracle. They had opposed the National Socialist Party during elections in the nineteen thirties. That put them on all the wrong lists. At the end of the war my father was held prisoner by the American Army. Doctors were considered low risk prisoners. One day my father managed to acquire a black minister's suit and white collar. Carrying a large spruce wreath, he set out on the two-hundred-mile march to join my mother who was living in a valley of the Alps. The disguise as a minister on his way to a nearby funeral served him well. Having grown up in a parsonage he knew the demeanor of a minister. He encountered military personnel from several occupying armies, conducted friendly conversations with them and regretted having to walk in a different direction at some point, never to be asked about his identity. His talent as a healer gave him opportunities to help people with medical advice and treatment in trade for food and shelter.

The joy of my parent's reunion was beyond description. Now they knew the war was over. For the previous six years my parents had exchanged daily letters, raw with emotion as one seldom finds between young lovers. It is only possible to understand the depth of these expressions of feelings when one considers that each one of these letters might have been the last one written, sent, or received. The Nazis were never mentioned in my parent's correspondence. They had developed mastery of subtext to an art form.

My father's life was threatened after he was sent from the war theater outside of Stalingrad to escort wounded soldiers and to return with a trainload of medical supplies after marrying my mother. When he returned to the Front, his entire medical unit had disappeared without a trace. Being without marching orders he was a deserter. This would have resulted in execution on the spot. By anyone. Especially dangerous was the German army. He went underground and never spoke a single word about his return from Stalingrad. There have been no known returnees from his medical unit after the war. They pledged, never to look back at the war.

My mother needed to find a safe haven. The Nazis had come to her father's church and carried off all of his books to burn them in the Town Square. He was warned not to speak of this event to anyone. This threat extended to his entire family. The valley where my mother found refuge was high in the Alps. The village is located in Austria but is accessible only from Bavaria. Her home was made in a converted barn. The village consisted of houses with balconies and flower boxes, sheltered in winter against the snow by large overhanging roofs. The road ended in a village square with a one room schoolhouse which served as an assembly hall and a small church.

My family had to leave this village after the war, because the French occupation government ordered all persons who had lived there for less than twenty Years to leave. The fact that my father was the only physician in the valley, did not matter. My parents went to run a home for children in the foothills of the Alps. My father was the resident doctor. Here I was born two days before Christmas.

Our father received a call to join the founding team of a new school near Köln. Our mother moved back to the Alps, a few miles down from where they had lived before. Here she spent her time combing and spinning wool, knitting and weaving blankets for barter or income.

This quiet activity was the time for our mother to tell us stories from around the world. She sang with us and accompanied these songs on her guitar. At bedtime she said prayers from her rich religious upbringing. We created feasts, especially when Papa came to visit during vacations and long holidays.

Fathers place of work was in a town that was still being rebuilt. It had been to 95% destroyed during the war. We had to wait until housing for families would become available. We were a refugee family like many million others. We felt like gypsies. We were looked upon by locals with suspicion. Our oldest brother was now the man in the house. Our oldest sister was the helper I became the seeker, the scout who was free to roam. I could find things our mother needed. Our father was our favorite guest, more like an uncle on brief visits. We loved his visits. There was delicious food. Cakes and pastries appeared. We sang, played music, went for walks with him, wearing our best Sunday clothes and shined shoes. Hugs, kisses and smiles. We were the perfect little family with children on their best behavior, a mother passionately in love with father, just the way he had been dreaming it during countless lonely nights at his tiny study away from home. When we brought him back to the railroad station, he left on the train waving. The train moved out of the station. He was gone. Then the tears came."

Now, half a century later this memory was causing me chest
pain and an unstoppable flood of tears. Why was I not able to
stop him from leaving? I now felt like a complete failure.
The image of my failure to find my father, to
bring him home now tore me up.

"There we were up in the mountains, a self-reliant tiny group of survivors. Mama provided three meals a day, nursing babies continuously for 22 Years until she had raised five girls and five boys. She looked very young. No one ever believed we were her children. Everyone took her for our mother's helper, a nanny or a teacher.

Back in the Alps, when I was seen walking for the first time. I disappeared for two and a half hours. I then I simply reappeared. I was ready to get away from the grabbing hands of grownups and walked into a world of discovery and wonderment. I had soon convinced my mother that I could be trusted to be safe outside and to find my way home. I wandered off into the hills, woods and valleys and began to discover everything this beautiful landscape had to offer. Wildlife left footprints for me to follow to grazing spots, showing me where deer would leave their kits in the middle of fields and dens in hidden places under oaks, pines and firs where small animals and foxes found bedding and shelter. I studied signs animals had left for me. I was fascinated by the dwellers of caves, rabbits, marmots, and foxes. I listened to their calls. I knew that I was being watched. I could hear the birds change their tune when I approached and calm down when they realized that I was not a threat to them. Further up the mountain free ranging cattle came over to see me sniffing my hands touching my skin with their cool wet noses or licking me with their rough tongues. Sheep were shy. I thought they were runaways. Foxes kept their distance. I was curious about holes animals dug and trees they hollowed out. I saw the piles of wood chips where woodpeckers lived. I observed the eyes of hunting birds, focusing on pray and swooping down coming up with something in their talons making high pitched sounds, struggling to carry the weight of the prey they had caught. In the Spring, raging rivers were carrying snow melt and rocks from the mountains to the valley. Seasons changed and buds came out and I watched deer browse on tiny green tips at the end of branches. I tasted them and found very delicious treats in sprouts of birch and beech that were spiraling out of their tiny protective buds of winter. l loved tasting the soft, light green spring needles of larch trees. When I came home, I told my mother about my discoveries. She had grown accustomed to live her life outside the house through my stories. She enjoyed my reports while she was home doing crafts, watching my siblings and nursing a baby.

One early Spring day, a neighbor was returning from the Village. The snow melt had crashed through an ice dam and an enormous wave had taken down trees and with huge chunks of ice. The flood tore away the foot bridge of the trail to the village. To make passage possible, a forester cleaned a tall tree that had dropped across the raging stream. People were crossing this wild water balancing across this tree. The man found me in the middle of this log. I was headed towards the village. He balanced towards me, picked me up and took me under his arm to return me to my mother. Everyone talked about the raging river. No one asked me where I was going. Another day I wandered off singing a little tune saying: Good bye I'm going to papa's town. I walked too close to a wild beehive. I was stung 32 times in the head alone. Once again the focus was on the bee stings and not on my song or my destination. Finally I succeeded in making my way to the railroad station. The Station Master saw me board the train. He knew who I was. He had seen my family during our teary-eyed goodbyes. He knew I did not belong on that train. Instantly he boarded the train, found me and carried me to the door. He jumped off the moving train with me under his arm. He put me down on the platform and told me to go home. I was two and a half Years old. I would soon forget my quest for finding my dad. I continued to expand my excursions, to see the valleys beyond and climb up to see the next set of mountains on the horizon. I liked to climb to the summit or follow streams to see where they would lead me. My journeys of discovery took four to six hours every day. Rain or snow did not slow me. I was at home in this world. Neighbors said I owned it. I learned to tell a fox track from a dog track, a rabbit track from a snow hair print. I became familiar with bird song even though I did not know their names. I knew when they were telling each other that I was coming. I felt very secure in the knowledge that many eyes were following my every step. I was never alone. As I went, I took in features looking back, doing a three hundred and sixty degree turn at road crossings. Using visual memory that has never failed me. Looking from mountaintops into the folds the landscape became "readable" to me. I watched fishermen catching trout with swishing flies, tied to long loose lines. I saw the beauty of the artfully crafted "flies", carefully placed in their special pouches. I saw the catch and could imagine how great the meal would taste. I cannot remember conversations with people I encountered in the wild or in the village. I hold the image of people looking at me and nodding. "Yes, you belong here. It's ok. You can watch. You want some lunch?"

I was surprised when I saw a new baby boy at home one day. Our mother had been very sick during his delivery. She decided to return to civilization. She laid claim to a house that belonged to my father's family near Frankfurt. We were getting ready to move again. Three hours train ride closer to our father, but still three hours away from him. With this extended time of separation from us, our father never had a chance to find out who we were. Saying goodbye to this world of mine was particularly hard. My curiosity won out and made it seem exciting."

Now the memory of the loss of my world tore me to shreds and the flood of tears would not stop. My mind began to wander towards ending my misery. Loneliness and despair were winning over my joy of life.

CHAPTER SEVEN

GRANDFATHER'S TOWN

"The move from our alpine village to a small town proved to be full of challenges. I was leaving the safety of wilderness and moved into a world of fast automobiles, machines and stone houses, occupied by people, who were always in a hurry.

The endless separation from our father was getting hard for all of us, even though we had no idea how it would feel not to be separated from him. Our mother was overwhelmed with four young children. She had suffered a very dangerous medical condition during her fourth delivery and was happy to shorten the distance to her physician husband. She had claimed the vacant living quarters of a small winery that belonged to my father's family, located between the rivers Mosel and Rhine where my grandfather was the minister of a Protestant Church. Our belongings were loaded on a wooden hand wagon with children on top and me trying to help pull the load to the station. I felt the excitement of a new place and the thrill of discovery.

I was nearly three years old. If Gypsies could do it, so could we. We felt a kinship with gypsies and loved their skills with musical instruments. The Gypsies in turn liked to stop by our house. We were friendly to them and ready to share what we had. We were outsiders just like them. We sang a beautiful song that describes a Gypsy family on the move, coping with the breaking wagon, mother carrying her babies while holding up the load. In this new world I was testing the nature of People in fast moving vehicles by stepping into their lane of travel to see how fast they could stop and how soon I could make them smile again. My last try of this game was with a motorcycle which could not stop or swerve. The rider stuck out his right leg and knocked me onto the pavement. A scar on my forehead has been a visible reminder ever since.

I was three years old when I suffered a third-degree burn. The pain I experienced was great enough to bring me close to fainting. What I retained was fearlessness from pain or physical discomfort. This surprised people I encountered later in life. In wrestling, in sports, during street fights or in my response to attacks, I experienced something strange. I was not scared. I was not afraid of pain. Pain could not even make me mad. I was unafraid of people. My opponents often thought I knew something or had some secret skill. They considered me dangerous. It made them hesitate for a split second. Hesitation is a big mistake during physical confrontations. It was in my nature to talk people out of violence, rather than having to deal with the messy consequences of inflicting pain on them."

Now in my memory the pain was back. It was driving tears into my eyes, causing new flooding, uncontrollable, unstoppable. I was feeling betrayed. Home was supposed to be a safe place.

"This accident should never have happened. It started for me a new realization: Inside the house was more dangerous for me than outside in nature or with total strangers. Here my instincts were protecting me. I was not relying on people in charge of keeping me safe.

I was now three years old. My mother had started to cook something on an open coil hot plate when her "helper" came to the door and distracted her. To keep me safe, she placed me in my brother's bed on the opposite side of the room, because this hot plate was sitting on a shelf above my bed, ready for a pot to be put on it. As soon as my mother had left the room, I left my brother's bed and returned to my own. I had to investigate the wire that led to the device above. To see better I pulled hard on the wire to cause the hot plate with its white-hot open coils to slip off the shelf, flip and land on my left thigh. I knew I was in trouble because I had disobeyed, so I stayed silent until my mother could smell my burning tissue. She ran in and removed the hot plate. Too late. I was already going into shock. I had suffered a third degree burn on the outside of my left thigh and a second degree burn on part of the outside of my left calf below the knee. Once the pain set in, I screamed for eleven days. I screamed every time something touched my leg and every time I moved my leg. Fortunately, my father came and dressed the wound with a one-inch layer of cod liver oil paste. This prevented the tissue from drying out and thereby prevented scabbing and muscle shrinkage.

This experience taught me that I can faint when something gets too painful. It is also possible to give in to pain and to welcome unconsciousness instead of fighting it. Even though this event went into hiding in my memory it changed my relationship to pain. I was no longer afraid of pain or physical punishment. It did not reduce my sense of caution or risk avoidance. It eliminated anticipatory dread and feelings of fear in me. During confrontations with others, I was able to stay very calm and did not get upset when I got physically hurt or injured. I developed an ability to be very focused and precise in my movements under extreme stress. Also, extreme stress caused my perception of time to be altered. It even changed my perception of movement. I was observing movement in slow motion. There was no more flight or fight response. Instead, I began to respond to stressful and upsetting situations by going into a very calm state.

On the slopes surrounding our new village were vineyards, cultivated here since Roman times. Old farm houses were equipped with micro wineries and cider presses. The house we lived in was no exception. It had a central courtyard, paved with cobblestones, fronted to the village main street by a huge stone wall with a solid gate, large enough to let harvest wagons in. At three sides of this foursquare were the house and utility buildings housing presses, bottling machines and wine making equipment. Underneath were large cellars, containing wine barrels and storage vessels. A stairway with a vaulted masonry ceiling led into these cellars and people tried to discourage me from going down there by inventing monsters who were supposed to be living there. What they did not know was that I was a friend of such spiritual beings which no one could see. When I found one of these doors open, I went inside and waited for my eyes to adjust to the dark. Now I could visit the monsters myself. I was in the habit of befriending spirits and creating protective partnerships with them. The dark was my friend. I was able to bring the dark with me wherever I went. Others were afraid of the dark. The dark protected me from the eyes of the night and from the eyes of people who were afraid in the dark. I used to laugh about people with flashlights. They blinded them and gave away to me where they were, I knew all that was to know about the wine cellars under our house and about the ghosts. The grown-ups were the ones who did not.

Opposite the gate were our living quarters with an elevated first floor. Bedrooms were upstairs. Out back were stairs leading down into a large garden where vegetables were growing. A path led further back to a gate which opened to orchards bounded by a barbed wire fence. Beyond the orchards was the fast country road. The fence was no boundary for me and I respected it mostly to humor grown-ups. One day I was near the fence, when a column of United States Army vehicles stopped, so they could steal apples. With sign language they asked for my help to stand watch while they stole apples from our orchard. When they were done, they thanked me and handed me a huge, sealed chunk of cheddar cheese. I ran it into my mother's kitchen where it was received with wonderment and gratitude. Cheese was still in very short supply and very expensive to buy. This was a five-pound hunk of cheese.

I had admiration and curiosity for people who made things with their hands and people who were good with the use of tools. I especially liked people who enjoyed what they were doing. I could spend hours watching a blacksmith, a mechanic or a cobbler. I liked observing the sounds and smells that accompanied their activities. I would listen to their stories and remarks about their world. They liked to talk about other people in town. Which ones to watch out for and which ones were ok. First, I went to find the ones to watch out for. I wanted to know why others were afraid of them. I preferred to see for myself what they were doing, how well they did it and what of their activities could be helpful to our own household. Also, why people did not like them or why they were afraid of them. I rarely found merit to the fear people had for others. To me it meant that they did not know them. In our new town two characters stood out:

The mayor, who was known to be scary, nasty and unfriendly. Everyone tried to avoid him. I made it my business to meet him and to become his friend. I succeeded. I had access to his office to play under his desk and to use his paper and pencils whenever I happened by.

The other one was the crazy, dangerous wild man behind the tall chicken wire fence, that was topped with razor wire near the end of town, who ran the scrap metal yard. He was guarded by a huge junkyard dog that protected this scary man and his junk. Horrible stories were being told about this mad man. I went to get to know him and to make friends with him and his killer dog. I figured, that no one would mess with a friend and the family of the craziest, maddest, most dangerous man in town. I found that to be true.

The Winter after we arrived was one of the coldest winters in this region on record. Our mother had written to her grandfather and mentioned the acute shortage of heating fuel in our community. He sent a railroad car full of coal. According to our mother's instructions, the coal was handed out to the freezing towns people by our crazy and dangerous junkyard friend, even- handedly and free of charge. It saved the town from freezing that winter. I was no longer roaming hills and dales in the mountains, but I continued to be the scout, who located things our household needed from bread and cheese to salt.

My earliest memory was a hot October day during apple harvest, when the dry, dusty heat made me desperately thirsty. I was walking towards our home where apples were being pressed for juice. My mind was focused on the gigantic vat full of cool apple juice fresh from the press. This vat was located in the left-hand corner of the courtyard. A small set of steps were built into the wall behind the vat. There was a little niche in the wall where a tall glass for sampling juice was kept. It was now the target of my quest. My thirst was so big that I was planning to drink the entire vat one glass after the other. While the men were busy reloading the presses with crushed apples, I managed to sneak into the courtyard undetected. I succeeded to make my way to the top of the stairs behind the Vat, reached the glass, dipped it into the ocean of juice and filled it to the rim. I began drinking. By the time the second glass had disappeared down my throat I was unable to even think about a third one. I will never forget my disappointment of having to leave so much of the precious juice behind. I was full and only the memory of my big thirst remained. I never tried to drink the whole vat again."

Unbelievably, the memory of this disappointment now made me flood by the side of the road, with as much liquid, as I had swallowed apple juice that day, soaking my shirt. Emotions rose in me raw and unforgiving. I had to turn around and find a dry shirt so I could continue my day.

"New modern things were to be discovered here in the civilized world. One day I found a piece of paper money. I decided to find out what it could buy. I went to the grocer and asked for a small candy bar, not knowing what the denomination of the money was. After handing me my candy bar, the clerk filled an envelope with bills and change and sent me home to give this right away to my mother. I did. I was unable to explain how I had gotten a candy bar and all this money. I learned something: Money could multiply when you bought a candy bar with it. Soon thereafter I had a chance to investigate coin money: When we visited my grandfather, I found a silver colored coin about the size of a nickel. I had disappeared and my mother's youngest brother, a regional ski champion, was sent to find me. He intercepted me close to town and found this coin in my tightly clenched fist.

"What are you doing with this money?" He asked.

"I wanted to buy ski," I answered.

The wonder years were coming to a close and the future was beginning to overlap the present when another child arrived. We were now a family of one girl and four boys. Living separated from our father was beginning to be untenable for our mother, who was sick and tired of my father sending her patients as helpers, thinking that my mother would have a healing influence on them. All they really accomplished was more work for my mother and putting her children at risk. I remember that she was getting very irritated by this arrangement. I heard her tell someone:

"By the time I had three children, I was maxed out." She now had five children and one on the way.

CHAPTER EIGHT

CITY

"Housing was never going to be resolved, unless our mother took matters into her own hands. She decided to move us into temporary quarters at a former hospital in town.

This would serve as headquarters for building our own home one and a half miles distant. Again, we sang our Gypsy song that describes the breaking up of camp and moving on. We felt the closest kinship to people who had no home. We knew that all of Europe and the World was filled with people who had been displaced, had lost their loved ones, their countries and their homes. We met them everywhere. We were these people."

The loss of place and friends now brought deep grief to my heart. Another home abandoned, friends and things left behind.

It was causing more flooding and left me feeling afloat with complete loss of control. I am sitting by the side of the road, feeling the loneliness of one who was never given the chance to be normal like everyone else. I never spoke a local dialect. "You talk funny. You talk like a radio announcer." People would say. I am so isolated within myself that I am completely unable to speak my thoughts or feelings. I have no language to describe them. All this loneliness is compressed in a dark place deep within myself.

"My life now became metropolitan. This was to be our final destination. New skills were required. New challenges arose and we were about to achieve something that we had been dreaming about for as long as I could remember. We were finally together as a family. Living with our father in one and the same city. It was the stuff of dreams come true. We were ready and motivated to build a permanent family home. I was stoked. Both my hands would be involved. I was given an extra year off before first grade. There was a world to be explored.

Our house was to be built on a piece of property that came with a ruin from WWII, in a neighborhood where most of the houses had been destroyed by phosphorous fire bombs and explosives. We were surrounded by burned out ruins some of which had not completely finished collapsing, making it all the more exciting to do archeology in these ruins of war. Off limits to children of course, we had no idea what that meant. I took to being in a town that was ninety five percent destroyed recently and now under vigorous reconstruction like a fish takes to water. There was a positive spirit, typical for the inhabitants of this city, who had lost everything. They were left with their lives and became known for their tolerance and great sense of humor. I found it easy to befriend them and to become one of them. No surprise when I was told that I have Neanderthal genes in me. Neanderthals had lived in this region 45000 Years ago. I felt at home here. The Neanderthal in me was now being let loose. This was the construction project I embraced with the enthusiasm of a homeless person, trying to come to rest. This was my kind of place.

I had walked the hills, the woods, the streets and the vineyards, now I was ready to dedicate myself in the construction of something permanent. I was now five years old.

While living in the mountains I had spent most of my time with people much older than myself. Perhaps this had made up for the fact that my father was only home for short visits. The grownups in my life were mentors, not friends my own age. There was not enough time for me to develop friendships with neighborhood kids my own age. This was about to change. In the past, when my mother invited local children over to make lanterns to celebrate a birthday or to attend one of our bonfires, I was seeing myself as a host, not as a kid looking to make friends. I wanted them to have fun. Fact was, that my world had grown much bigger than theirs and I had no language to share my experiences with them.

Moving to this city had not been easy. We took the train with much too much luggage and once again, with no help. At the station, our mother succeeded in loading everything onto the train: Babies, toddlers, children, luggage and all. When the stationmaster blew the whistle and she reached for me to shove me into the door I had wandered off. There was no time to find me without missing the train and losing the others and all of her belongings. She had to choose. Trusting in my Guardian Angels and hers, she boarded the train, believing that somehow I was going to end up where I belonged. The train was picking up speed. The stationmaster saw me and grabbed me under his arm, jumped on the step of the accelerating train, opened the door, shoved me aboard and slammed the door shut, before jumping off at the very end of the platform. I walked forward until I saw my family.

"There you are," my mother said, her voice aquiver doing her best to hide the fact that she was beside herself with fear, sick to her stomach and trembling the thought of me alone on the platform had brought her close to fainting. She managed to pull herself together. She did not want to frighten the rest of her children. She knew how to look tough in extreme situations.

Giving birth to a child every other year, finding temporary housing, completing one chaotic trip after another and now finally moving to a huge city to reunite with our father after all these years of separation, was a momentous achievement. Living the drama of life with a very large and growing family after surviving the war and dealing with post war stress was one thing. Making and finding needed supplies not always available in stores was another. Generating the mental strength not taught in schools and developing patience only found in Saints, were things our mother accomplished on her own. Diapers made of cotton had to be hand washed, air dried and reused. Everyone was tired, exhausted and traumatized. Seeing her, you would never have known it. Spinning and weaving woolen goods, knitting garments, making and embroidering clothes for her children and nursing babies all the while, that was our mother.

She was excited to have finally succeeded to step with her flock into the same town as her husband. Her faith and her loyalty were stronger than all the obstacles she had overcome. Her deep universal exhaustion did not prevent her from taking charge of the next steps. Finding a home site. Designing a house with the help of one of her cousins who was an architect. Getting plans approved. Staking the location of the dwelling. Finding construction financing, negotiating with contractors, demolition and removal of the old ruin on the property. Supervising construction, hooking up utilities with another child on the way, one nursing and one on her hand. All these steps would make her dream come true. Building a house for the family after years of forced separation from her beloved husband, thousands of letters written and received. Six children and another one on the way, moving them into a picturesque, quiet neighborhood surrounded by forests and farms, overlooking the valley. Hope and patience were finally being rewarded. The property my parents had found was a quarter pie shaped piece of land located half an hour walking distance through a beautiful forest from the School where our father was working.

For me this was a new world to discover. It contained a little bit of everything I knew something about. Forests, a brook, steep hills, wildlife, farms, a village-like residential neighborhood plus one new thing altogether: Friends my own age. All this made me feel right at home. A four-Season venue made to suit all of my interests. Great for sledding in winter or letting a scooter run too fast in summer. This city is a long drawn out string of small towns, housing a rich palette of industry, art, music and theater plus a great opera house. The town is built on both sides of the river and up the steep flanks of the valley. I was now ready to grow up. My parents had given me one extra year to roam. I used it to build my own buildings and community after I was done cleaning thousands of recycled bricks."

CHAPTER NINE

A REAL FAMILY

"This world now included the beloved man whom we had missed so sorely and who knew us mostly from his short visits. He knew us as happy to see him, a polished smiley faced family in freshly pressed Sunday clothes and holiday spirits. Now it was time for him to discover who we really were. He now had the chance and the challenge to learn how this family functioned and what his place was in our little tribe, compared to the family he had invented in his heart and mind during years of separation. That was true to his relationship with our mother also. Father finally had an opportunity to find out what it meant to have a family. He finally saw with his own eyes what our mother's every day was like. He was about to experience that it is easier to become a father than to be one. As far as I was concerned, he had no idea what my role in our family was and how he could fit into this world. Our father was not the alpha male in this pack.

Our oldest brother was. Father now had to earn his place at the table. He was slowly waking up from a dream about a family you could visit once in a while, into the waking state of a family, that did not go away. This family would be there day in and day out rain or shine. Sickness and health, smiles and tears for better or for far, far worse. This was not the family any more, that he could walk away from to return to his little study, where all of his dreams were born. It was a real family now. And the war that had broken out inside of him about this reality soon became visible.

Like our mother our father came from a minister's household. From parents who had survived two world wars, who were burdened by the philosophical heritage of the nineteenth century. This society was transitioning from parents who owned their children and raising them with an iron fist, to an era in which women and children began asking for more individual rights. Women had kept the home fires burning, while men went about fighting wars that no one could understand or properly explain and certainly not justify. The confusion was multi layered. Corporal punishment was still used to discipline children. Obedience was a strictly enforced rigor in most households. Military discipline models were used to enforce rules, but lacked the urgency of combat survival. Women had been raising their children unimpeded by their disciplinarian husbands, without imperatives that are normal in the trenches of combat. This outdated model of raising children was now being altered in the Halls of new schools. The new idea was to create a collaborative artistic approach to education. It was something women understood, even though the experience of the role of their own fathers was leaving them with the conflict of accepting the old, while wishing for the new. The two sources of reference our father had to children was his own parent's parish with a strong and willful father and a subservient, kind and endlessly patient mother, born from a family of ministers going all the way back to Martin Luther. The other was the school, where his influence was dedicated to a newly evolving education model. He found himself placed in a newly freed country full of hope, guided by a holistic approach to developing free individuals, commitment to guiding children to achieving the best of their potential, which they were seen to be born with. He had made a commitment to restore freedom of speech and expression, freedom of education, freedom of medicine and the quest for a new social order, that would guarantee and guard these newly won freedoms. All these ideals were packed into one mind and one heart.

Now came reality. We had existed and resided in the ideals of this heart, where his new family was born. The real family came as a shock. He had never lived with a household full of children who were dirty, snot nosed, needy creatures, that did not go home at two o'clock in the afternoon to the custody of their own parents. We were persons who were not always glad to see him and who did not always obey. We were babies who were screaming when they wanted or needed something. There was a wife who was suddenly first and foremost a mother and only now and then a lover. She did not need to be told how to run a household. She was no longer the eighteen-year-old he had married right after graduation. While he was not looking, she had become a fully-grown woman who had managed to raise her family without his help. And she was with child again. She commanded respect that females in his former life never dared to ask for. He had no clue what all of this meant.

Here, next to this man stood I, five-year old. Up to this point I had walked out of the house unrestricted. I had been free to roam, to explore, to discover, to learn, to meet people, to make friends and to tell my mother about my discoveries at the end of each day. I had grown fearless and knew how to find my way home. I woke up early every day, ready to be immersed in whatever the world had to offer. I was the boy who more than once had risked his life to find this man, to bring him home. Now I saw this man look at me and say to my mother:

"Mother, we have to tame this boy." I had no idea what this man was talking about. Later that day, after I had been physically punished for not being where I was supposed to be when I was ordered to be ready, I asked my mother how this was to be understood, what I should make of this. She looked at me and said simply:" At home, fathers have permission to do that." I was curious what she meant by this. This was not part of the order of my universe. The finding out process was about to begin. It became clear to me that the search for my father was far from over."

The memory of this tragic moment and the betrayal of a perfectly good child by his father, who had no clue who his son was and that it was not his job to domesticate, train or to save him, was shredding me to bits and pieces now. This was the man I loved. What the hell was he talking about? Why did he not just go ahead and kill me right then and there? Instead he interfered in my life and forced me to react to mistakes not of my own making. Now, thinking about my unsuccessful search for my dad made me flood again. I never found him during his lifetime. Memories kept streaming, flooding me, exhausting me, making death more appealing than life.

"The construction of the new house was taking the front seat in my daily life now. I was given an extra year before I was to be enrolled in school. The hilltop settlement where we built the house was called Mountain Peace. Foundation work and wall construction began. My great grandfather sent truckloads of very hard bricks he was able to salvage from war ruins. My first construction job was to hammer the old mortar off of thousands of bricks. I was tireless. I kept at it until the entire pile was clean. I was now six years old. I loved this city. Our new city is said to be the most tolerant community in Germany. There are more religious organizations living peacefully side by side here. People are known to laugh more and are happier, even though it drizzles or rains almost all the time.

"We have the fire and the sun inside of us", someone told me. I witnessed the rebuilding of this City from rubble. The transformation from rubble to a vibrant place for people was astounding. To grow up, live, work, and play, the people of this town built good schools, art galleries, theaters, an operahouse, concert halls, plus a wonderful zoo. They even built an Olympic size swimming pool shaped like a clam shell and named it "the swim opera". The town was kept safe by a police force that proclaimed to be everyone's friend and helper. This vibrant economy could build value and everyone had a job. The usual nonsense of political life was met with a great sense of humor. Service to one another was the rule. Corruption was the exception.

My mother took me to the farmer's market downtown next to the City Hall one day. I used a mobile restroom but was unaware that it had exit doors on both sides. Leaving it I got turned around and left through the door on the opposite side of the vehicle. Everything looked alike but my Mother was not there. I waited for a long time until a woman noticed that I looked lost. She took me to the "white mice" as everyone called the traffic police because they wore green and white uniforms and drove white vehicles. Once inside the station I was asked by an officer to tell my story of how I got lost and where my family was living. These nice officers even shared their lunch with me. Then they took me in their large beautiful white BMW eight-cylinder police car up the hill to return me to my family. The way we found the address was by my description of the features of the area including intersections of roads and vegetation. I was new to everything and could not recall any of the street names. I had good visual memory. It was helpful to find my house. After verifying that the young woman at the door was indeed my mother, they left me in her care and returned to their duties.

A few days later I walked back downtown, found the police headquarters and decided to visit my new police friends. Secretly, I was hoping to get another ride in that wonderful police car. They did feed me lunch again and drove me home. The officer told me this time not to come visit again.

"What if all the kids in town came to see us, how could we do our work?" This made sense to me. I never went back. I had a good relationship with police, law enforcement and first responders ever since. The wooded area surrounding our new home was four square miles in size consisting of a rounded hilltop where our settlement was surrounded by steep terrain with washouts and folds. This was our four-square mile wooded playground. Or our sovereign country if you had asked us then. These woods were littered with abandoned and partially hidden war equipment, ammunition in green gray metal containers, machine guns, unexploded phosphorus bombs and other explosive devices that made kids curious and far too often went off and took their lives. To help with this problem call stations had been erected. Located where people could press a lever and report such finds. The city had the munitions removed by experts. The police were our friends and helpers in deed. Of course, first we tried to see if we could set them off. Or fire the guns. Then we reported our find.

Together with my new friends I took possession of these woods. Soon we knew every tree, every stone, every fence and every feature of the land. In parts new trees had been planted and the terrain was mostly impenetrable to grownups other than the foresters. Surrounded by construction activity it came as no surprise that we diverted materials to build our own tree houses and a fortress on my property with a flat roof as a look out and a secret trap door at the bottom. We also built camouflaged underground shelters in strategic locations for us to be safe and to have hiding places and defenses. We even had stoves made from cinder blocks. My best friend was the son of a couple who ran a home for single young men aged eighteen to twenty-eight from Southern Europe. Turks, Greeks, Yugoslavs, Italians, Spaniards and Portuguese all working in construction jobs rebuilding our town. There was also a hostel for city teenagers to spend summer vacation time outside of town in Nature during the Summer. My friend had learned a lot of wrestling and close combat moves from these tough young men. Even though we did play a lot of war games, we did not tolerate the use of weapons like bows and arrows. Conflict with kids from downtown often were settled in one on one fights between gang leaders. This way disagreements were settled and ended quickly. No harm was done. Our territory was mostly respected. I was acting diplomat, since I considered physical confrontations to be only a last resort after negotiations had failed or we had been attacked without warning. My friends and I were well prepared. We practiced defensive warfare. We thought like martial arts experts: First talk the opponent down. Failing that, disable him. Use real hurt only as a very last resort. We were defenders of our own world.

We could disappear in our woods not to be heard or seen in mere seconds. Surprise was always on our side. We distinguished between the native vs. cowboy ways of doing things, preferring the native ways because they required total integration in nature, while rejecting intruders who came often armed and did not know where they were. This was done easily. If they did not see us, we scared them off before they had a clue what was spooking them.

I remember one summer day when a city group of kids came to roam and play in our area. This in itself would not have raised an eyebrow, had they come unarmed. Instead they were carrying bows and arrows which made us watch them. Unfortunately for them they decided to destroy one of our underground shelters next to the Pond of Dead Cats. We were upset about their leaders who were grown-ups. A young woman and a young man in their early twenties. We thought they needed to be punished. We grabbed members of their gang one by one and rolled them in a bear hug down the steep bank. This bomb crater was used as a dump on one side and filled one third with murky water. We let them go just in time to roll them into the smelly water, which made them go home. The ones who did not decide to go home voluntarily were told to go home or else. They did not want to find out what 'or else' meant. Out of this little dirty pool ran a small, well fed stream of water. Now we had to deal with the grown-ups. The lady was taken prisoner first. We tied her by her wrists behind her back and fastened the long end of the line to a small, bent down birch tree, which gave her movement but no chance to escape. The male leader who stuck around as expected was first blocked from interfering, then tied up with wrists and ankles connected behind his back. We placed him face down in the flowing water so that he had to raise his head to breathe. To capture the grownups, we had literally dropped on their heads from our hiding places in trees above the trail. This made them lose their balance and fall over like dead trees. Rescuers soon arrived at the scene. No one had been able to get a good look at us. We were still there observing but we had disappeared. No one got hurt, except the egos of the grown-ups. (Years later I walked this area with my daughter showing her my childhood playground. To my surprise, we actually found visible signs and some of the parts of an underground fort: Stove pipe, cinder blocks and an indentation in the ground. The trees had since grown up and the entire area is now a beautiful city park.)"

Memories of this wonderful world and my amazing friends flooded me with heartbreak. I missed them. I had lost track of all of them and had never been able to reconnect. I now felt alone and isolated. My pain was mixed up with my emotional distress. I was punishing myself for being irrational. I could not forgive myself for taking a passenger into a head on collision with me.

Chapter Ten

THE HOUSE

"Building the house was pure heaven for me. Cleaning mortar of used bricks and observing workmen. First demolition crews, then surveyors, diggers, masons, then carpenters. Architect and contractors interacting with my mother who was in charge, a child on one hand, baby in the other arm, nursing. Once in a while she had to run into town to talk to officials about permits, deal with administrative obstacles and to see about more financing. Often, she was given valuable tips by city employees after their supervisors had left the room, which opened to her sources of reconstruction financing at very low interest rates. Helpful was my great grandfather who never missed an opportunity to send the right building materials at exactly the right time. I suspected that the architect was instrumental in this miracle. I cannot remember my great grandfather but I know I adored him and I admired how he was there for his family. He and my great grandmother had a loving tone and demeanor with their families. I think my father was intimidated by them for reasons I could never understand. We never went to visit them, which I would have loved. This side of our family was all hugs and kisses when they greeted us and each other and when they said goodbye. This was my Eastern European family. They called me Sunny. I loved it when some of them came to visit, to see the progress with the house and to count how many children we now were: Eight with very young-looking parents.

The house was nearing completion, the roof was decked in and mechanicals were being installed. One day in the Fall our mother decided, ready or not, we were moving in. It was a major improvisation but this was her victory march. The architect and his wife came for an improvised meal and our mother told them that she had no wine. They said they would bring wine. Bring glasses too, we do not have wine glasses either. We laughed about our kind of hospitality for a long time. During that party, there were no windows or doors installed yet. Our mother moved us into the unfinished house despite the fact, that it was late November and most of the windows had not arrived as promised, can only be appreciated by looking at the long list of obstacles she had single handedly removed to get us there. Winter was upon us. The only space with heat at this point was a tiny garden house, which had its own canning stove. That is where we went to get warmed up, where hot meals were prepared and where the family was gathered for our first Christmas. We were singing Christmas carols. There was a knock at the door. After the reply:

"Come in and Merry Christmas" our next-door neighbor walked in with a huge tray of pastries fresh out of the oven. A welcome, that made us shed tears of joy.

This, I thought, is the true Christmas Spirit. Soon thereafter the house had windows and doors. The furnace was up and running and everyone was hoping for their own room. The house was now habitable, even though it was still far from finished. Our parents gave a party for the workmen. The masons and carpenters were jolly with songs and jokes. I had never seen that many bottles of beer before. I can hear the song of the carpenters to this day. When most of the beer had stopped flowing and everyone had gone home, our neighbor's boy and I saw the big vat of leftover potato salad. We could not resist to do a little cooking of our own. We collected all the leftover beer and poured it into the potato salad. We got caught stirring the delicious brew. Getting caught in the act of wasting perfectly good food got a big response from our two fathers. "The hide was pulled over our ears". Two fathers punishing two boys. We knew that our sentence was well deserved. There was one curious difference about our reactions. The boy from next door screamed at the top of his lungs, while I took my punishment without atwitch or a sound.

Finally my first school year was here. In my opinion, I could have been in school all along. I could not wait. Our school was not new to me. We had participated in festivities at the school as a family and being the children of the school physician and teacher, everyone knew who we were. "You must be one of them" people would say, putting their pointing finger on my chest. I did not appreciate to be known like a pink poodle. I resolved to live my life like it was a public event."

CHAPTER ELEVEN

LIFE IN THE CITY

"The first school year was here. Was it scarier to see the proud parents disappear or to dare walking into this monster building that began to swallow up many hundreds of students. Will anyone come out again? I was an insider because I had siblings and a father in the system. I was very happy to finally be a student. I took my role seriously as one who knew the school well and was able to help new classmates find their way. We were 52 students in my classroom. Every morning our teacher welcomed each one of us at the door with a hand-shake while making direct eye contact. We then recited a poem together after everyone had found their chair. This is how the class came to order.

"My world in the woods was replaced by activities around school and around town. To make better music, my home-made garden hose and kitchen funnel horn was replaced with a real French horn. Bow and arrow were replaced by a cello which I shared with my older brother. I was invited to join the Youth Concert Society. Student members were permitted to occupy vacant seats at concerts, the opera and the theater. Music was a constant in our house. In our music room we had a grand piano. Our aunt Rosi played the piano. She had a huge repertoire. She taught flute and piano at our house. Also a famous singing coach came to our music room with her professional opera singer patients, to help them repair their voices. She played the scores of many operas. This way we heard a lot of music."

The memory of these days has laid a soundtrack into my soul. On a normal day, this was a wonderful gift, as I could play music in my mind at will. Now in my injured mind, it caused me to feel pain of the loss of yet another world.

"School was a major daily event. It began in the morning with the mayhem of getting everyone fed, dressed and ready. Our father was very well prepared to teach his classes, which were lauded by his students as some of the best lectures they had ever heard. He was as nervous before school as a performer before a public performance. Having to deal with his flock of frantic children made him lose his temper. Yelling and threatening us was not helpful. It resulted in nervously misplaced school books, forgotten sports attire and missing homework. Even different shoes on right and left feet. I tried to keep to myself during such moments, by being the first one out of the house. The way to school was steep downhill run for a mile and a half through a forest. The therapeutic effect of the walk through these woods calmed everyone down again. At school, my teachers created a discovery tour of the world in concentric circles, starting right here in town, with fairy tales and colorful artwork to tell the stories in pictures. This was the way we were introduced to activities of the steel industry and to innovation that was going on all around us. We learned writing by developing our own reports. All of this felt good. It was a continuation of my early discoveries in the mountains.

With French horn and cello, I ventured into the city to take lessons. I made new acquaintances and forged friendships. I became involved in activities that were permitted by my father. Some things had to be done on my own time. I freed up my time, by running from the house to lessons and back, saving one hour each way to see movies, which was prohibited. I enjoyed concerts and the theater. I was still the scout of the family with no restrictions in my mind.

My father strongly rejected the lifestyle I had brought with me from the mountains. I did not have his structured sense of time. I met appointments more out of respect for other people's time then out of discipline. After seven Years of freedom I was not able to, or saw good reason to change my ways. My excursions during my life in the woods now transformed to life with my new friends which continued after school. After lunch I found myself walking by the front door. Instead of turning towards the music room to practice cello or horn I wandered out of that door for the rest of the day without thinking of what anyone might be expecting me to do. My father for one. I respected and loved him. But his agenda was not part of what my life was calling me to do. I had adopted my own group of mentors over the years. Now father was new to my life.

Now I needed time to learn how to work his plans into my life. There was no dialogue in my mind and no language to steer my thought process. What made things worse, was that I was not afraid. This was my world and I intended to play in it. I received some punishment for missing meals or practice. This did not bother me and it did not put a dialogue into my mind like:

"You have to remember to do this or that, or else." Outside was still my safe place. The worst things that had happened to me in my life so far, had happened inside the house. This made my outside excursions attractive, even though they earned me the title of 'runaway'. I was told that my father came home every day and ate lunch. He then went to his study in the attic to rest. Once he re-emerged, he went about running his family business. He checked on our practice of musical instruments and sometimes even checked our homework. Then came the daily question: Where is Sunny?

The best answer anyone had besides "I don't know" was: "He went that way". Now I had it coming: Late for dinner might result in a lock out. It is easy to use a lock out as punishment for a person who depends on the house for shelter and comfort. It might have worked on any of my siblings. I was not such a person. I had constructed at least six shelters around the neighborhood in trees, underground and above ground. I could get cozy in five minutes no matter what temperature or weather we had. Being denied entry to the house was a favor. It gave me permission to spend time at my own place in my own world. Out here I was safe. Locking me out was unsuccessful in creating remorse or forcing obedience. My father was frustrated. He began reacting to my strange behavior: He became violent.

I finally triggered reactions so big, they were only comparable to violent thunderstorms. Severe punishment was becoming a regular event. In my eyes, such punishment was never in proportion to the offense. I regarded it as a natural disaster. My father would take me into the coal cellar and find a gnarly piece of firewood. He beat me with it. I did not twitch or guard, because that only caused his rage to increase.

I entered into a different state myself: I was now an outside observer. I saw him appearing besides himself, while I was feeling to be beside myself, watching the beating of my body as though it was happening to someone else. I did feel the pain, but it did not bother or frighten me. During these moments, I felt empathy for him. I was hoping that he would snap out of it soon.

Suddenly these episodes were over and he simply walked away. I never felt upset. I might have been stunned for a while. No one was able to explain this to me. My mother continued to stand by him. She seemed to think that this was normal. She was used to explosive outbursts like my fathers' from her own dad, the minister who had similar unexplainable episodes of fury, triggered by unrelatable events. I had a strange relationship to pain. I could feel it, but I was always able to isolate and observe it. I had no fear of pain and did not react emotionally to it. My ability to hold still and not to twitch in reaction to inflicted pain made these episodes seem less severe than they were. I was more puzzled than upset. My love for him remained undiminished.

Asking my mother about this strange and for our family very unusual behavior, she replied:

"Fathers have permission to do this". I took it as: "Father has permission to do this on our property". Soon this was to be tested. When our mother was preparing to have another baby, my father and his older children went on a two week long hiking and camping trip. It was very hot. We were all tired, thirsty and hungry. Exhausted, our oldest sister sat down by the side of the trail and began to cry. We needed to rest. We all agreed. Except our father. He marched some distance ahead of us. Then he turned back and approached our oldest sister with threatening gestures and words. This was almost as bad as someone threatening our mother. My brothers and I stepped into his way. We denied him access to our sister. The posture we took towards him was leaving no doubt in his mind, that he had to go through us to get to her. Out here, were the little family that had grown up together without him, ready to defend each other. Here we were not on his property. We were on our own turf. Different rules applied here: Ours. What he saw in our eyes made him stop. He turned around and walked away as if nothing had happened.

For me, episodes of violence happened with increasing regularity. No one ever talked about it. Here was the kindest, gentlest, most loving man whom I could move to tears with an adagio from one of Mozart's French Horn concertos or a Schubrt string quartet, suddenly transformed into a raging beast and then just as suddenly he would simply return to his gentle self. (Years later I went to see him to confront him about violence. He had absolutely no recollection. I believed him. He had untreated PTSD.)

Even in my mother's eyes the beatings I was receiving had to stop. In her desperation she bought a thirty-foot long chain and with it, she locked me to a radiator in an upstairs bedroom after school. I did not fight her. I would have used the chain to defend her. She did this to make sure I was present when my father came home or when he woke up from his nap. For now, the beatings for running away stopped. The use of a chain was one link closer to my heart than what my mother had intended. It seeded in me a desire to get away from this family. I no longer recognized it as the one I had grown up in. What we had become in the mountains, had vanished. This was not my family. I was quietly and deeply offended.

I had a strange problem. I had to keep my distance to avoid getting into confrontations with my father, that could have hurt him and by extension my family. It was my distance that set him off.

I soon discovered some unexplainable traits in myself. One episode during my early school days demonstrates this best. One day in seventh grade I became upset with a couple of big burly twins from the eighth grade who were bullying my classmates. Especially smaller ones. I decided to confront them.

"Why do you always pick on small kids? Don't you have anyone your own size to pick on? Why do you take their lunch money? Don't you get enough to eat at home?" Then I challenged them:" Come on, you frightened kittens, pick on me." I followed up. "Ten o'clock break in the middle of the school yard."

"Hahahaha, the two of them replied. You'll be ours!"

"Ten," I answered and went to my classroom. When we met during the ten o'clock break. I said quietly:

"There is one thing you need to know about me: Remember I play the French horn. Do not hit me on the lips. Also, do not kick me. That could make me mad. Otherwise you can fight me any way you want."

"Hohoho" Answered one of the twins and without hesitation in one fluid movement, he kicked me right in my mouth. This triggered something in me. It caused my perception of time and movement to change. Movement suddenly appeared to be in slow motion. My focus was razor sharp. A few seconds later I had completely disabled him. The bully was on the ground and his brother was no longer interested in helping him. He now had his hands full to carry him off to the doctor's office.

My opponent missed several weeks of school, recovering from injuries he had suffered. I could not recall any details of this fight other than the onset of the time warp and that each of his movements was answered by a reply, using his forward momentum against him. None of the many students who were crowding around us to watch the fight and to keep the teachers from interfering, could tell what had just happened. It had happened too fast. Everyone had only seen the kick to my face. Neither of the twins ever touched another classmate of mine again.

Our school developed rich theatrical and musical programs. Some of our teachers were composers and poets giving us an opportunity to present their new work on stage with the orchestra and during public music festivals in the great Concert Hall of the City. I knew this venue well.

French horn in hand, wearing a beige trench coat over an immaculate suit with white shirt and tie and polished shoes plus an assertive attitude, I had begun to walk with other musicians through the musician's entrance into this concert hall, pretending to be one of them. I would drop my coat and horn at the coat check and walk to the front and center seating area, selected a prime seat that was left empty. No one ever questioned me. This seemed a long time from the early days up in the gallery when we attempted to shoot love notes with rubber band slingshots from one side of the concert hall balcony to the chosen girl on the opposite side only to have some of them fall short and land in some ladies teased up hair. We enjoyed observing with glee her puzzled look when she retrieved and read the love note that had landed in her "nest".

Music was an approved after school activity for me. The time required to practice and to go to lessons and rehearsals had to be used wisely. I ran to most of my appointments, saving precious hours to do activities of my own choosing. Speed of travel was essential. Using skates in the winter was not so good for the cello. I fell several times when I hit a bare spot. I was ok, but the neck broke off my cello. After a while, the instrument maker stopped charging my parents for the neck repairs. I can remember the sweet smell of the pipe he smoked while gluing the neck back to my cello. At school I was playing the French horn in the orchestra for stage productions.

On one occasion we were about to play an original composition and to my dismay, I discovered that my mouthpiece was not in its place. To get it, I had to run the mile and a half home, arriving back at my chair just as the lights went down. I grabbed my horn tightly and unfortunately broke all three valve operating strings. When my big solo came, I remember when my heart began to race. Then I lost consciousness. When the performance was over, the composer came to see me. He congratulated me and said that he had no idea the horn solo could sound this good and that he was very thankful for a job well done. I had played the whole thing without valves and to this day I have no idea how I had done it.

Our new hometown gave me many cultural and social opportunities including listening to- and playing jazz. I was four years too young to be admitted to jazz clubs. I was spending my "City time" with people about six years older than myself. I hid in plain sight.

At home, I helped moving large rocks building a retaining wall for a terrace. I suffered a hernia. It did not get repaired until I stated, that it would end my music career. Once the hernia was mended, French horn playing became a professional pursuit for me. The French horn represented freedom. It paid for travel and saved me from confrontations with my father. I was slowly moving myself forward and into my own world. It was a mental process at first that had begun slowly and ended up making me independent like a magic carpet, taking me away to fourteen countries before my teenage years were over."

CHAPTER TWELVE

END OF THE DREAM

"Suddenly, after only a few short Years in our new home, my parents announced that our family was to move back to southern Germany. I had no idea why they had to move and I was absolutely sure that this had nothing to do with my life. This only confirmed to me that I was done with this family. To be sure: Not with my mother or my siblings. They were my real family and I would have laid down my life for every one of them. If I could have asked them, they all would have said no to this move."

This memory was killing me now. How much more did I have to endure? Why did my entire life spool in front of my mind's eye? Was it not hard enough to live my life? To stay alive? Why did I have to go back and look through this negative filter, turning everything

into a total disaster? At home I felt disconnected. I saw myself to
be the source of every problem. Fatigue was overwhelming me.
"I must end this", I said to myself. "I must end this useless
life. The world will be better off without me."

"Leaving my new found home left me numb. I was just getting my
life into a comfortable pattern. I did well at school and was surrounded
by many wonderful friends. This was a betrayal on my life. This move
eliminated all the credits I had earned academically and socially except
for one: Music.

Absurdly, I found myself helping a professional painter to remove
all signs of my family's life from our house to get it ready to put it on
the market for sale.

Moving the family to southern Germany was a huge enterprise.
We had taken ten years to dream up this life and to build this home.
It took another ten years for this dream to go up in smoke. I was upset
enough, that I did not want to know or to remember details. It seemed
to me, that my life line had snapped and I was adrift. Everything to do
with this move was more complicated, took longer and cost more than
anyone had expected. I knew that my mother's heart was not in it. For
ten years, she had pursued a dream and now we were walking away
from it, just like that? I did not think so. She too had lost her compass
and her anchor. She was too busy and we all went into a crazy time as
if we had been hit by a tornado that scattered us to all four winds. The
house we called home was finally sold.

I began to realize that I was thrown back into my former search
for my father. The man who had just ended my life was not the man I
had been searching for. Over the years of separation, we had managed
to invent the man we loved as he had dreamed for himself the perfect
family we could never be. Everything to do with this move was
ridiculous. Inadequately planned, hugely underfinanced plus lacking
transparency of reason. My family had been ignored and disrespected.
We had developed a better sense of loyalty than this. This was not ok.

I wanted nothing to do with it. I coasted, tried to ignore the details and remembered nothing. Not even where I slept. Yes, I helped to move our large library. Yes, we moved it into another temporary shelter in an old farm house and yes, I learned how to drive at age fifteen, using my oldest brother's license after a vigorous test by my mother. I drove the VW bus to chauffeur my family, when no one else was at hand. In the beginning, our housing situation was completely up in the air. I had no idea where anyone was staying. I had been temporarily sleeping in my father's medical examination room at the new school. When I was interviewed in this room by the eighth-grade teacher, I treated him as a guest in my house to the effect, that he could not see how I could possibly fit into his classroom of smart, but much less mature students.

The school decided to move me up one grade from the first half of eighth grade to the second half of ninth grade. That was a terrible decision at a time when I was busy restarting my life in a new world. I had not even begun to mourn the loss of my life and all my friends. I was in unspeakable distress and wanted nothing to do with any of this. Skipping a grade ended my academic career. In Germany there was no meaningful place in society without a doctorate degree. You had no voice and your fate was sealed. You became a worker bee.

I had to reinvent myself. Music was my refuge. Our complicated improvisation of a confusing life was in my way. Everything was temporary again but this time there was no visible goal. Socially, I was now completely isolated and could only relate to one boy in my class, who had welcomed me the first day I set foot in the school yard. Some premature rebel-teenagers with bad reputations thought I was cool. Cool was not what I wanted to be. The class I was moved up to was (of all people) my own father's home room. This was a comic tragedy or a tragic comedy. I was not even interested to find out which. I disliked everything about this misadventure. There was no reason for me to be there. And every reason to be elsewhere. I could not let myself get involved in this town. Restrictions imposed by my father included visits to restaurants, cafes, nightclubs and places where normal teenagers gather to have fun. Also forbidden were organized sports because there might be former Nazi coaches on staff. To end the constant gossip about my whereabouts, I decided to go everywhere within one hour, using a bicycle. I made sure that I was seen. I also had classmates spread rumors that they had seen me in places on opposite ends of town during the same hour of the same day. That ended this problem. My father listened to these impossible stories about his son being everywhere at once. He never believed another rumor about me again.

There was one exception. I had permission to join the European Alpine Club. This provided the one and only highlight for my existence. I was getting instructions and training from a rock-climbing coach who ended up taking me to a limestone climbing rock after extensive classroom lessons in the use of climbing gear and in survival techniques in alpine environments. When we arrived at this popular climbing rock, we noticed a party ahead of us. The lead climber was on top, standing braced with his foot against a small rock, holding a rope in his bare hands which was tied to his partners chest in a slip knot. She was hanging limp with no hand or foot hold engaged, depending on her lead climber with her life.

For a second this picture reminded me of my family and our move to the south. My coach grabbed some gear and ran up the backside of the rock to belay this woman and her lead climber. After securing the rope of the distressed climber in the wall, he took over control. He dropped me a rope. I stepped into it and following his instructions, I went up behind the climber in the wall.

Talking to her calmly, I was able to reassure her of her safety. I found hand and foot holds for her to descend and succeeded to talk her down. We were relieved to see this day come to a good end.

"Now you know what I was talking about." My coach said. "There is no exception to being prepared. There is no such thing as an easy rock or a safe climb. This was a potentially fatal error on the lead's part. There was not another minute to spare. He would have dropped her to her death on this harmless little one hitch practice rock. Take this lesson to heart."

I did. I read a lot of survival accounts. Arctic, Antarctic, Himalaya, and our own Alps. A welcome distraction amid my shredded life.

We were planning a trek into the Alps. I was in need of good alpine gear to be able to approach the very mountains I had seen in the distance when I was a child. I was getting excited and animated. My friend from class was coming along. On this trip, my coach was going to accompany us for a few days while we were climbing the German side of the Alps up to the border. Then he was going to turn back.

Living with my family temporarily in a village south of town put me in bicycle distance to a landscape company. Here I was able to get a job to earn money to buy the best boots and mountaineering gear money could buy. When it was time to travel, I was properly equipped. I was about to return to my childhood world in which I felt like I knew every rock, every tree and every river. This was going to be a hard trek. It was also going to save my sanity. Was I going to find my lost life? Could I forget about my father and start worrying about myself? Could I do this alone? Looking up to the mountains made me feel like I could breathe. That was a good start."

Chapter Thirteen

THE TREK HOME

"Accompanied by my friend and my coach, I began our trek with a small tent, down sleeping bags and down parkas into the Alps. My heart beat in anticipation. Once we gained altitude, everything looked very familiar to me and I felt life returning into my veins. We parted ways just below the pass from the Bavarian side of the Alps to the Austrian Alps. Our coach shared some last-minute advice. After taking one long, longing look into the distance, where we were headed, he said his goodbyes and turned back. The view of the Mountains in the distance was stunning. My friend and I went on to cross over to the Arlberg massif and on towards the Engadin mountains. I felt like I was connecting with my life again. I could finally breathe.

After leaving our coach behind, we climbed the pass to the border, then descended the serpentine trail down towards Landau in a very fast descend like mountain goats, as an alpinist from Austria had called it, after observing us coming down the mountain towards him. We felt the exhilaration of speed and the anticipation of ever higher mountains before us. We both did not speak much. We were in a hurry to get to a river valley to make camp at a place where I had been once before. A couple of hours up the valley was an excursion café. I had been there and met the owners the last time I was in the Austrian Alps. I had become friends with their son and the entire family. Here is what happened.

The family who owned an excursion café in a valley a half day walk up river south of town had a fourteen-year-old son. He was a top fit teenager who spent his winters skiing and summers hiking when he was not working for the family. Here, he was the mailman, shopper for restaurant supplies and helper at the café. He was also the stand-in shepherd for livestock his family kept on summer pasture up in a side valley. We were camped in a meadow by the river near the café using a Lapland style teepee tent with a fire hole in the center.

This early July day a sudden rainstorm delivered a deluge of water to the valley causing the river to rise over its banks. When the first snowflakes appeared, the owner's concern arose for the safety of the animals at their summer pasture. They told me that animals would walk away from the driving snow uphill, until they lost traction and fell down. This had to be prevented by heading them off and driving them back to the shelter of the trees. The other concern was the safe crossing of the river for the rescuers. Only a person very familiar with the river could attempt a crossing under these conditions. Today, the boy was dispatched together with the shepherd to run up and intercept the cattle and the horses on their way to the steep and dangerous slopes.

We were watching the rain and noticed the swelling river inch its way up to our campsite. Our fire kept us dry and cozy warm when we realized that our campsite was going to be flooded soon. We had to move to higher ground and it was getting dark. We tested the wet ground on hands and knees until we had found a flat high spot the size of our tent base. Relocating our gear, setting up the tent and getting the fire moved to the new location took some time. Soon we had everything warm and dry again. The rain had turned to snow. Later that night, the owners of the café came over to talk to us about the rescue at the mountain pasture.

"We have no heat at the cafe and the way it is snowing we are concerned that our men will be freezing cold and soaking wet when they come down. Would you let them take shelter in your tent next to the fire to warm themselves and to dry out?"

"Absolutely," we replied. "We have warm blankets, towels and sleeping bags. We will put a pot of water on for tea." When the shepherd and the boy finally arrived at the cafe, the owners were relieved. The boy was extremely exhausted and close to fainting. His core temperature had dropped. He had gotten doused by icy cold river water several times on the way down. After the crossing he was completely spent. The shepherd had carried him back to the cafe.

We immediately stripped off the boy's wet clothes and replaced them with our own dry warm cotton shirts and woolen sweaters. With the shepherd's help, we laid the boy on top of a sleeping bag by the fire. The shepherd also changed into dry clothes and moved the boy from facing the fire to having the heat reach his back, making sure that the warming process was slow and even. We had become more concerned, when the boy stopped shaking uncontrollably and just lay limp and still. We kept checking his pulse and breathing. He was unresponsive for what seemed to be a very long time. What we were doing at this moment was all that could be done. There was no other help. No telephone and no passable road. We rubbed his arms legs and chest with our towels and kept rotating him by the fire. When he finally came to, we gave him little sips of peppermint tea with honey. The day before, we had gathered wild blueberries, bought sugar, butter and freshly baked bread in town. We had made cold stirred blueberry jam to go with sweet cream butter on toasted bread. We were happy when finally the boy was ready to try a taste of this special treat. The shepherd told us about the rescue at the mountain pasture:

"Once we caught up with the animals, they were moving uphill as we had expected. I was staying below, calling them, while I sent the boy to race uphill, pass them, before they reached the rocky terrain where it was getting steep and to turn them around. All the while it was getting slippery in the driving snow and visibility was very poor in the fading light. As soon as he was above the animals the boy began to turn them around. When I heard the first bell of the lead animal, all I could see were white and gray shapes moving in a white and gray slope. Once the boy had found all of the animals and they could hear my voice, he prevented them from turning back up. They all reached the shelter of the trees near the river. Here they will stay now and wait out the storm. The boy had fallen into rivulets and puddles of icy water. By the time he reached the river where I was waiting for him, he was exhausted. We still had to go back across the river and walk back to the café. Crossing the swollen river was treacherous. We had to stay close together, holding on to each other's sleeves, while I was searching with my boots for the stepping stones, now submerged under raging water. The boy suddenly slipped and fell. Luckily, we had just reached the other side and I was able to grab him by the collar of his jacket and pull him up to safety onto the river bank. One more time this night he got completely drenched in ice cold water. He was now too cold and too exhausted to walk. I had to carry him all the way back to the café. Thank God for your fire. There is no heat at the café. Look at him. Tough as nails. He will make it."

When the boy came around, he was able to take sips of tea, try a taste of our blueberry treat then went into a deep sleep. We were watching over him until late into the next day. The Storm had passed and all was well.

When we arrived at the café this time, we were welcomed like family. We were invited to go up to the valley and spend some time with the shepherd.

"Maybe no snow storm this time", they mused, smiling.

"No tent with fire this time either," I chuckled. We accepted the invitation enthusiastically.

The following morning, the shepherd led us up the trail.

"We want to help you with the chores," I told him.

"The cow will kick you", he said, "do you know how to milk?"

"Yes" I said.

"No", said my friend simultaneously.

"If you show him, we both can." I suggested.

"We will climb above the tree line. It is an Alpine pasture. We have twelve Haflinger horses up here, thirty-two heifers. And one cow."

"How long have you been doing this?" I asked.

"All my life" he replied. "My parents died in an avalanche. This family took me in. During the winter season, I am a ski instructor and in the summer, I live up here."

"Don't you get lonely?" my friend asked. "I am never alone up here. Wait until you see."

I knew what he meant. My friend had no idea what the shepherd was talking about. He would find out soon enough. We reached a small footpath down to the river. Here was the famous crossing. Stepping stones visible this time. The trail was almost hidden by vegetation, up the river for half a mile, where a small brook entered theriver. Here, the trail turned and followed this brook. I scooped a handful and tasted the water. "Good" I said.

"This is our brook." The shepherd said proudly. We walked through pines, firs, birches, larches and a variety of small bushes azaleas and blueberries. Soon we entered a boulder-strewn grassy bowl, that was laid out like an open hand pointing up to the sky. It was rimmed on two sides by steep rock spires with short rubble fields at their base. I remembered the descriptions the boy gave when he ran up here to stop the cattle from scaling these walls.

Now there was a brilliant blue sky and the summer sun was burning my skin. I was getting hungry. In the center before us was a rock wall, polished and dark. Water shedding over it in white frothy streaks. The air was still. I could hear the breathing of animals nearby. Some chirping of small birds.

"We are almost there." The shepherd said. "It's right over there." He pointed to the right. All we could see, was grass and big boulders. "There it is. That's the hut." We saw two extra large boulders. A narrow entrance was squeezed between them. There was a door. We dropped our backpacks to the ground. "Come in", he said. A room was dug out towards the back and reinforced with dry laid rock walls, defining a step and a rock paved platform. It smelled like fresh soil. There was a built-in wooden table, a bench and a full-sized bed with mattress and

73

blankets. Shelving to the left, holding cooking utensils next to a cast iron stove on top of which sat a very large cast iron frying pan. A nook in the wall held some papers and a couple of books. To the right were some wooden shelves for garments, boots, raingear and a couple of coat hooks for a duster and a hat. It looked surprisingly neat and picked up. Off to the side were the milking utensils and a milking stool.

"That is a real cowboy hat", he pointed out. "I told you. In the Winters I am a ski instructor. A student from Texas sent the hat to me. "You are a real cowboy now," she wrote. "She did not believe my story about my summer job. That is part of the problem. We look sharp in ski gear. Girls look good too. They come to play. Sometimes the heart does not want to let them go. I belong here. No woman would live in this cave. No shower, bathroom or dishes. Just a few forks and spoons. One big frying pan. You want a bath, you go up there." His eyes pointed to the big rock wall. "Cleanest water in the world. A shower too. You step under the little waterfall. You cannot see it from here. The water is ice cold. You boys go up there and look around. You can set up your tent over there, behind that boulder. I will make you a snack. Later we milk the cow and then I make us some dinner. We all eat from the big skillet. No plates. Everyone gets their own spoon." He stuck out his hand to my friend. "They call me Joe. For Joseph.

"Tom," my friend said. "For Thomas." Neither of them big talkers.

"Sunny for sunshine, I chimed in, laughing.

"Welcome to my home. Tomorrow you look around the area. The next day you can carry the milk down to the valley." After thanking him for his hospitality, we began setting up camp, went over for a delicious sandwich, had a tall drink of milk, then finished building our alpine home. The air smelled of soil, grass, sage, and a very slight whiff of cow – and horse manure. It was very quiet. We went up the grassy slope to inspect the waterfall-shower. We could see the sun lighting the flanks of mountains across the valley. When we came down to the hut, the Massif was fully aglow in the afternoon light.

"Not bad for a campsite" Tom said. "Look ", he pointed. I saw snowcapped peaks to the south lit by the afternoon sun like white glowing lamps.

"These are the twelve thousand-foot mountains of the central alps."
Joe said.

"Ahh ", I stretched luxuriously. "This is where I belong. My body
likes it here. It feels like I have come home."

Dinner from the large skillet was delicious. Milk rice with cinnamon
and a good helping of sugar sprinkled over it.

"Dig in", Joe said. "I made hot chocolate, I thought you kids would
like it". We could not have been happier. Early next morning after
breakfast the shepherd told us to carry a block of salt to the salt lick near
a gravelly drinking spot by the brook. The animals came to inspect the
new-comers but kept their distance. We noticed how smart everything
was arranged and how shy the horses were. They knew that we did not
belong here. For now, we waited for them. We had some sugar cubes in
our pockets to make a good first impression.

Finally, one late morning I was laying on my back, watching eagles
circling on the rising air currents, when the lead horse came over to me
and breathed right into my face. She let me touch her soft nose and I
blew some air into her nostrils. I found my sugar cube and placed it on
my open hand. Carefully the horse nibbled on the sugar and picked it
up. The treat soon brought the other horses over. We were now accepted
as part of the mountain community.

Our explorations took us into a new world. Once we had managed
to find a passable way around the wet rock we scrambled up and stepped
onto the first rock shelf which was a natural dam for a pond of clear
almost black looking water. I saw the perfect reflection of the mountains
with blue sky above slowly changing as we walked around the pond.
It was perfectly still. We tried to make no noise with our boots. We
acted like we had walked into a sanctuary. I noticed water feeding
this pond at the far side. A second rock step with water streaming
down its face. We were curious about its source. As we climbed, little
waterfalls were reflecting light making rainbows in the fine spray. We
discovered a second pond formed by the shape of the bedrock which was
holding it. To our surprise the water was now aquamarine in color. The
temperature of the water seemed colder than that of the pond below.
Vegetation around this pond was sparse, hugging the ground. White

and gray rock faces reached up into a perfectly blue sky. More water coming from above was feeding this pond inviting us to investigate further.

We climbed up to a third dam and found a third pond. This pond had milky white colored water. This place looked like sculpted by a glacier. The ice melted back and was now revealing rock faces polished and sculpted after pushing loose rocks off to the sides with large boulders challenging intruders like us. This pond looked like a shot of pernod in a glass of ice-cold water. Walking around the shore we reached the source of the water. The bottom of a small glacier hidden from the sun on the north face of the mountain. It seemed tired of scrubbing rock and glad to finally show its work to us.

The wild beauty of this hidden treasure was stunning. There were no trails up here. The view to the valley presented three ponds in three different colors. This was something only the human eye can fully capture all at once. We stood gazing at the alpine panorama and the blue sky above. We were barely able to breathe. We sat and spent a long time in silence. Breathing taking in the scent of aromatic mountain herbs and feeling the icy water on our bare feet. Washing our faces drinking the clear water. Finally, quiet as though we had just attended a religious service we climbed back down. We were still speaking in whispered voices when we saw Joe.

Now we were ready to deliver milk to the valley. It was harder than we anticipated. The stiff milk container did not have a padded back brace like modern backpacks. We took turns but noted how strange it seemed that working people would not change this immediately but were willing to put up with this pain and inconvenience year after year. We spoke to our hosts at the café in gratitude about this invitation and told them what we had discovered up in the mountain.

This was my kind of world. We did resolve to use one of our packs to carry milk next time."

These images now appeared in my memory. I felt the loss
of my life as it should have been as it could have been, had
I not gotten snared in someone else's life that to me was
unacceptable. I was at a loss. How had I become a person
who seemed willing to live with no control over his own life?
I was unable to see a way out other than to terminate it.

"Nature was my place. Here I felt at home and now I was going to
leave once again.

"Why did you leave you fool?" my mind was now asking me. "Our
parents are selfish and do not regard their children's life worth another
look." My friends all agreed.

Such dark thoughts accompanied my return to the reality of
everyday life. I returned with the resolve to find my own life somehow.
School was no longer holding my attention. Deep in my mind was a
notion that something was going to turn this around. I was sure I could
trust my life. I had to prepare myself for something new."

CHAPTER FOURTEEN

MUSIC

"A highlight during my short time in the new town happened during a
surveying field trip designed to apply mathematics with added botanical
and geological courses in the Bavarian Alps. The landscape seemed
very familiar to me. I was having a feeling that I had been here before.
I looked at a map and realized that we were just on the other side of
the mountain where I had been roaming as a child. I had come full
circle when I arrived at the other side of my childhood mountain. That
evening we had a celebration. Together with a classmate who was a
gifted dancer, we did an improvisation. Modern dance with Cornet. A
classmate let me use his cornet, which has a sweet and soft sound. After
the dance, I told my partner that I had not thought about what to play
but that I had played what I saw her dance. She said:

"Funny you said this. I did the same thing. I danced what you
played."

Fusion accomplished. The class loved it.

The following summer I won a French horn position in a stage orchestra for an international theater and music event in Switzerland. A series of Seven uncut performance cycles of Goethe's Faust with music and dance performances. Amazing musicians were playing in this orchestra, raising the quality of our performances to a very high level. I was immersed in music. At age fifteen, I was the youngest member of this orchestra. Dressed in my tuxedo, I managed to be admitted to a nightclub where we saw The Modern Jazz Quartet and The Dave Brubeck Quartet with Paul Desmond. We were introduced as fellow musicians. This sent me over the moon. I became a much better French horn player during this Summer.

"I must get out of this school or it will suffocate me." I announced. I reached an agreement with my parents. If I can get a scholarship, I will go to study French horn at the Music academy. I will enroll at a high school as a guest student. I can live in the attic of my relatives house, ten minutes walking distance from both schools.

I won the scholarship. I now had a chance to participate in concert tours coordinated by the Cite Club Universitaire de Paris to several locations in France. At Anjou we celebrated the re-consecration of the Abbey of Fontavraud, where Richard the Lionhearted is resting and to Cap D'Aille near Monaco, where we spent a summer giving televised concerts with French soloists. Also to Paris, where we were exposed to art. A Youth Orchestra from Germany accompanying Soloists and Choirs from France in televised performances. These opportunities were created to rekindle friendships between French and German youth, speaking a common language: Music.

My studies at the academy ended when I was accepted to the Bavarian State Conservatory where I studied with a famous French horn professor.

I spent a Summer at the Collegium Musicum at Schloss Weissenstein in Pommersfelden Bavaria playing chamber music and participating in a concert series with musicians from all over Europe. This was another event created for musicians from many countries to create friendships and to support understanding using our common language, music.

I participated in a European Concert Tour with the Camerata Academica of Salzburg under the direction of pianist Geza Anda. I was invited to sit in with the Hungarian Opera Company during their Germany tour of the Gypsy Baron by Johann Strauss.

Finally, I was engaged in a South African Symphony Orchestra playing the second French Horn. I was now eighteen years old.

To learn the English language, I had brought with me a book written by South African author Lorens Van Der Post: The lost tribe of the Kalahari. He had given this book to me when he was visiting Germany for the first time after the fall of the Nazi regime to give a speech on occasion of the publication of this book. The author Sir Laurence had been a guest at our house. I now had this book at my hotel room open on my desk where I spent every free moment copying long hand all 360 pages, looking up and copying down the words I had forgotten over and over. I had arrived in Durban with very little English to my command other than "how do you pronounce this" and "what do you call that" and most importantly: "I need money". These were excellent conversation starters for me. I spoke to the lift operator. He was member of the Bantu tribe. I was impressed that he could speak four languages fluently. Some of my colleagues told me that in evolution blacks were just one degree above monkeys. To find the truth I expanded my excursions in and around town. My colleagues were very generous, driving me around the outskirts of town, showing me the sights. I saw everything from dude ranches to Bantustan, the one room house settlements for native workers, sprinkled over entire hillsides. My hosts missed no opportunity to point out their own superiority.

Early one morning I heard a chorus of about twelve voices accompanied by a steady rhythm. It was hauntingly beautiful. Thinking it was some music festival I leaned out of my fourth story hotel window to take a look and to get a better listen. It turned out this was a road crew of about twenty-four men digging a trench down main street towards the City Center. They were advancing by having the last person walk forward as a fore singer. This was his rest period. Once he arrived in front, the next person took his place to be the lead. The rest of the crew answered in perfect harmony and in perfect pitch. (This sound was made famous by Ladysmith Black Mambazo sponsored by Paul Simon.) A problem began to surface now. I could not speak to my colleagues about my experiences. As I have done all my life, I went everywhere to see things for myself. The Chinese market, the Indian market, the Bantu market and the Zulu market. When I mentioned these excursions to someone in the orchestra their eyes widened and they tried to convince me that I had put my life in danger. I continued my exploratory walks, but stopped talking about it. My colleagues were more comfortable with their own opinions than with facts. I was not about to argue with them about things I saw with my own eyes.

One afternoon, I wandered along the shore following foot trails hidden in tall grass. Suddenly I could feel a complicated rhythm vibrating in the soil under my feet. I followed this sound and found Zulu warriors in brilliantly colored beaded war attire engaged in a dance, snaking and circling in many variations. I was spellbound. Seeing me like this, one of the chiefs waved me to come closer. He explained that this was a Zulu dancing competition. He invited me to sit and join him as one of the judges for the event. I was witnessing very sophisticated choreography of dances performed to hauntingly beautiful harmonies by many voices and drum rhythms coordinated to perfection.

I heard of the tale told in history class of white schools. When the first settlers arrived on the Cape, it was uninhabited. I found a Nazi regime practicing Apartheid. I was shocked to learn that white police were a threat, not people I visited and spoke to. This is how afraid the 2% minority of whites appeared to be behind their white fences with their heavy monitored gates and their white painted iron bars.

I was now walking with my head low and my heart in deep distress. A beam of light was an upcoming concert featuring Rachmaninoff's piano concerto #2 performed by a pianist from Brazil. While we were rehearsing, I was watching a Bantu worker varnish woodwork above the gallery opposite the stage. We had been struggling with a transition in this piece. When we finally got it right and before the conductor could say anything, I saw the "Genetically challenged monkey man" on top of his ladder look at us as if to say:

"There you go, what took you so long?"

During a break, Musicians were discussing vacations. Someone said to me:

"When you have a little money saved up, there is a fantastic safari you can book. It is safe, comfortable and well equipped. You travel to Namibia to the Kalahari Desert. It is expensive but worth it!" He had my attention.

"What is the purpose of the safari? There cannot be much wildlife in the desert? Is it a photo safari?" I asked.

"Oh no, "he exclaimed," It is much better than that! It is a hunting safari. You get to shoot bushmen!" I looked around. Not one person in my company blinked an eye. I began thinking about what I had just heard. I decided to make harmless inquiries about the author of the "Lost Tribe of the Kalahari" book I had on my desk.

"Is that a book where people find out where bushmen live?" I asked the person who had promoted the safari idea. He told me that the author of this book was living in exile in England because he was a "Kaffir Lover" and that his book was banned in South Africa.

"You get caught with that book; you go to jail," he cautioned me. Fortunately, I had never mentioned to anyone that I was learning English by copying this book. I removed the book from my desk and made my notes disappear. I knew that it was time for me to become very quiet.

Even my conversation with a beautiful young lady I had started to date was now extremely guarded. She belonged to society in town. Together we were invited to many parties and events. I was paraded for the fast advance of my language skills, while I began looking for an opportunity to get away from these people and from this country. I no longer could enjoy playing music for people who had no concept of Human Rights other than their own superiority advantage and power. I was shocked to find myself in the presence of Nazis. This was not how I wanted my breath to be taken away. I began observing. To anyone watching me everything was exactly the way as it had been the day before. Every day after rehearsal I went to my little warm up room to practice. There was an upright piano in this room. I was working on Beethoven's French Horn Sonata when someone knocked at the door.

"Come in." I replied.

"Hello I am The soloist. I will be playing the piano concerto with you on Friday." The caller said.

"I am Sunny. Second French horn. I am happy to meet you and glad you have made it here safely".

"I am relieved. I hate to fly. It frightens me. I get vertigo. What are you playing?

"The horn sonata by Beethoven."

"May I?" He asked as he sat down on the piano bench holding out his hand. I handed him the music.

"Let me do a run through with you." he said. We played the piece and he was delighted.

"This was fun. Will you be practicing here tomorrow?" he asked.

"Yes, I will be here after rehearsal. You are playing with us at tomorrow's rehearsal?"

"Yes. I will see you tomorrow. Will you let me play with you again after tomorrow's rehearsal?"

"Of course. Thank you." As promised, he returned the next day after rehearsal. I tried to hand him the piano score.

"That's fine. I remember." We had a good time playing the sonata. He made some helpful suggestions about articulation. We talked about Europe. The pianist spoke about an upcoming ten country tour in Europe and about how he wished he had a driver so he would not have to fly all the time.

"I would give anything not to have to fly from country to country."

"I might have a solution for you". I said after some thought. Then I went out on a limb:

"Can I confide in You with a personal predicament?"

"Of course," he said. I told him about my concern of my unavoidable collision with the Apartheid Regime of South Africa. I told him how I had unknowingly taken a chance of being arrested and jailed for using a banned book to study English. I then spoke about my discovery of the killer safaris in the Kalahari Desert targeting the very same people that were the subject of my banned book. I explained that I was no longer enjoying playing music for these people or living in their country.

"I have to find a way out of here. If you help me, I will drive you all over Europe in return. I have a car there." The following day he stopped by my room again and suggested to meet me at a downtown café the day after the concert. He said that he was working with his Impresario on a proposal. When we met, he offered to advance me the airfare back to Munich via Portugal in return for my driving him during his next European concert tour. We would fly to Portugal together.

"It will be much to my relief not to have to make this long flight by myself." He gave me the itinerary for the flight to Portugal and told me that my ticket would be arriving at the downtown travel agency. This done, I was on my own until the following week, when after the Friday concert there were a few days off. My departure would be on that following Saturday.

Everything went smoothly until Wednesday afternoon. I had joined several musicians in the downtown arcade to go for iced coffee. The clerk of the travel agency in the arcade called out to me, asking me to come in for a moment. When I caught up with my colleagues, they asked me what the travel agent wanted. I told them that a flight to Germany had been booked for me and that I believed it had something to do with my family's concerns about our mother's pneumonia.

"She is seriously ill with pneumonia, which has ended my grandmother's life." I explained. The pneumonia part of the story was true. Hearing about this, the town manager offered to arrange a telephone call to Europe and I was grateful for that. When the call came through during rehearsal, I went to his office and spoke to my mother about our concerns for her life and that I was on my way to be with her. She understood subtext and calmed me down, saying that the emergency was over and that the family did not need for me to come home.

After returning to the rehearsal, I made the announcement of the good news to the assembled orchestra and everyone applauded. The following day we had a concert, followed by half a week off. After the concert, I checked out of my present hotel and moved to a tourist motel closer to the beach, for one night.

The downtown bus terminal was one block away from the concert hall. As I approached with my suitcase in hand, some musicians were standing there, waiting for the airport bus. I was praying that they were picking someone up, arriving from the airport. In my head I was already formulating another vacation story. Maybe Namibia, Killer Safari?

Their guest arrived and they left not five seconds before my departure. I boarded this bus undetected and soon was safely on board to Johannesburg. I must have been holding my breath until the plane was airborne. I took a huge breath of air.

"I hate flying too" said the person in the seat next to me. "Where are you going?"

"Johannesburg" I answered. Once in Johannesburg, I was met by a driver who took me to an apartment building. It looked like a soviet era slab of concrete gray and plain. The pianist and I were guests for dinner and for the night here, scheduled to fly off to Nigeria and on to Portugal the next day. Our hosts and the pianist were old friends. Being Holocaust survivors, they understood the reason for my escape.

The apartment building had outside balcony walkways on all floors leading to elevators and stairs. Inside the apartment our hosts had assembled an exquisite collection of rare African artifacts. I was in awe. My hosts explained that they were glad to help me because they themselves had been forced to flee their home land from the Nazis. After their arrival here in South Africa they had made a vow to each other, never to move again for the rest of their lives. They left the outside of the apartment as plain as they had found it and placed their treasured collections inside hidden from the world.

This collection was a rare documentation of artistic talent from all corners of the African Continent, assembled by a connoisseur of art. As a trader, our host had to travel the African Continent far and wide. It was a bittersweet moment for me to see the artistic genius of the many tribes and nations of this hauntingly beautiful continent and to realize that I was forced to leave. I was getting ready to continue the journey of my life.

I was now nineteen Years old.

The following day we flew to Lisbon where we spent a couple of days sightseeing and tasting the outstanding food, before parting ways.

Before leaving Africa, I had confided in one of my colleagues. I asked him to announce my departure at the next rehearsal and to call it an act of protest against the oppressive regime of Apartheid and its Human Rights abuses.

I asked him to declare that I was unable to play music for them because to me, music was an inherited gift and a common language for all of Humanity, never exclusive to one small oppressive minority. He promised to do this for me under one condition: He asked me to never reveal escape plans again. Not to friends, not to anyone.

"Make your announcements after you have reached your destination".

I agreed and promised."

Now in Maine, by the side of the road through the filter of my broken mind and heart, the memory of the end of my music engagement in South Afrika felt like a failure and yet another disruption and a tear in the fabric of a futile life with no future.

Once again, I felt as alone as I had in my hotel room after realizing that I could not stay in Africa. It evoked more waves of flooding. At home, just like in Africa, I now had no one to talk to because I simply could not reach out. I was alone. Right in the middle of people who I knew loved me. This was as hard for me to understand as it seemed impossible for everyone else to comprehend. Once again, I was now wearing an invisibility cloak.

"The promised Europe Concert tour took place. Wonderful moments were the reward. Hungary was still under communist regime. In contrast to the stark public appearance of Budapest stood the old concert hall and this outstanding event. Featured were the fifth Beethoven Piano concerto and the ninth Beethoven Symphony performed by the National Symphony Orchestra of Hungary. The hall had the most exquisite acoustics. The Audience was listening actively and the orchestra was performing with breathtaking intensity and passion as if to say:

"This is our heritage, this is our world, this is our language and this is not something anyone can suppress with machine guns or tanks. No Nazi sympathizers, no communists, no extremists of any color can reach us here. Here we are free." We spent time with ambassadors and the Russian culture attaché. These people had no clue about culture or the universal language of art.

Another outstanding experience during this concert tour was a ten day stay in Paris, where I was free to explore the town while the soloist was recording piano music for radio and television. I spent hours every day visiting the great art exhibits of Paris. I grew to love the work of Pablo Picasso, exhibited at the Grand Palais during the "Homage a Picasso". The opportunity to simply spend time in the presence of this great work opened me up to Picasso. This genius has a special place in my heart ever since.

The concert tour was a success. We said goodbye in Rome, after visiting Venice, Florence and Milan. The pianist was so enthusiastic about my company and the transportation that he offered to purchase a Jaguar E type for me to keep, provided that I made time to drive him during his future engagements around Europe. I had to pass on this offer. Our contract was complete and I had to move on.

While playing French horn in an orchestra at a Bavarian spa for the summer season, I had the opportunity to connect with members of my family and especially to spend a lot of time with my late grandmother's sister, who owned a café and B+B in this town by the lake where she was known for her legendary homemade desserts.

As it turned out, she was one of the very few people who could fully understand my heartbreak over my decision to leave South Africa. Before WWI, she had spent time in East Africa, where she and a number of her closest friends had made plans to build a new world free of social, racial, environmental religious or economic injustices, only to be forced to abandon this dream, when the First World War broke out.

We were having long and wonderful conversations. I had adopted her as my substitute Grandmother. She made me feel welcome in the arms of her family.

"We lost your grandmother in 1939, just a few months after the birth of her youngest daughter. Your grandmother was a saint." She said and mused: "Too many losses, too great a burden to carry. Life on plan B and plan C. Two wars. We had to be very tough. We were being crushed over and over. This here was our last refuge. I go for a dip in the lake every day of the year, summer and winter When it was frozen, your uncle cut a hole into the ice for me next to the dock. You can see I am tough. I had to be," she laughed.

During long conversations she was now reliving her memories: She told me the story of her dream of creating a better world in Afrika. Her Husband was part of her Africa group of friends. She never mentioned to me that he had died the year before. He could have been in the next room. Maybe his spirit was right there with us. All her memories came flooding fresh and raw. She was very animated as she spoke to me. Her story was one of bravery, love, generosity, vision, hope and tragedy. All that was left of their activities in Africa were her memories and the Glacier on top of Mount Kilimanjaro, which her partners had climbed and mapped. They even skied on this amazing mountain between Tanzania and Kenya. Her group was planning to prove, that it is possible to feed the world without poisons and to live together without injustice of any sort.

"The war ended all of this. We lost too many lives and all of our money.

Influenced by these conversations about what was happening to the world after all that had been sacrificed during her lifetime, I wanted to change my life. It was time for me to follow this call and to continue her important work. I decided to put down the French horn and study organic farming instead.

CHAPTER FIFTEEN

BACK FROM AFRICA

"There are plenty of musicians." I told her. "They will keep the tradition of music alive without me." She agreed. Our common concern was the health of the planet. Ever since reading "Silent Spring" by Rachel Carson during the early sixties, I was concerned about nature and the role humans are playing in preserving, protecting, or destroying our planet. I therefore decided to study Organic Farming. I wanted to find out if it was possible to feed the world without poisoning the planet in the process and by default ending life altogether.

I applied to do an apprenticeship on an organic farm in southern Germany, run by an inventor and pioneer in soil improvement, biogas generation and direct marketing. This farmer had a reputation of being tough and engaged. He had served in Parliament and cared about principled leadership. On his farm we produced certified raw milk, vegetables, stone oven baked sourdough bread made from homegrown flour, free-range eggs, poultry and organic beef. We marketed our products directly through stores, hospitals, hotels, health spas and served private customers with daily deliveries.

Leaving the orchestra to feed livestock, rising at quarter of four in the morning and working until eight at night with a one-hour lunch break, was both rewarding and challenging for me. I loved the early mornings and observing the first light. I enjoyed feeding the herd and nursing calves, grooming horses and preparing the next meal for the cows after letting them out to pasture after milking. It was a quiet time to witness nature waking up. I felt truly happy. This could be my life. There was a purpose. Physically it was hard for me to go from playing an instrument to twelve hours of hard labor each day. I was getting very sore. To endure it I had to pretend I was training for the Olympics. I found myself wrapping my shoelaces around my wrists because my hands were hurting too much to tie my boots. There was a rumor that I must have suffered a nervous breakdown and that I had come here for occupational therapy. Why would anyone in their right mind trade life in a tuxedo for horse and cow manure and twelve hours of hard work?

It took six months for the farmer, his wife and their friends to realize that I was as serious about creating a sustainable future as they were. I was ready to learn real farming. It was not a five-minute idea. I had bribed the foreman to translate my daily work orders which were given to me in heavy Swabian accent, first thing after the morning dairy was done and before breakfast. In the beginning I had no clue what the farmer was saying. I wanted to meet and exceed his expectations anyway. Finally, he saw my reasons for wanting to learn organic farming from him. He was a grower of humus, healthy soil, healthy plants and healthy animals. He was an expert in direct marketing of farm products. I wanted to see about a poison free world.

We were on the same side. Once he was convinced that I was motivated, he began treating me like I was his own son.

The following four Years I spent training with some of the most talented and accomplished farmers in Germany. This education included weekly classroom hours at state run regional farming schools, where I was the only student from Organic farms. I noticed that the literature used by the agriculture department was provided and written by the fertilizer and pesticide industries. Future farmers were being tested on information imparted by the chemical industry. Industries that were claiming that their chemicals were safe. They paid scientists to prove it. Our teachers were not so sure. One who taught these claims wanted to prove the truth about this. During a demonstration for farmers he used his bare arm to stir the mixture. Unfortunately, he contracted a disabling nervous condition that spread from this arm to the rest of his body. His doctor advised him to never touch or inhale these chemicals again. To us he said now:

"Use gas masks and protective clothing. Consider these substances highly toxic."

During the nineteen fifties and -sixties, herbicides, fungicides and pesticides were mixed, handled and sprayed by farmers without any protection. There were no warnings about health risks or the need for protective clothing. No warnings about overspray into the environment or risks to water and wildlife. This teacher was just speaking from his own experience and part of the problem was that his income still depended on selling these toxic methods."

Now in my vehicle in Maine I could feel the memory of this betrayal of the people who produce the food we eat and the families who suffer the health consequences, fall on me with its full weight causing grief over my failure to turn this around. Why was I feeling this? Why now? Where did these memories suddenly come from?

"Tell me more," my counsellor said. "How did this make you feel?"

"It made me very concerned about a generation that was obedient and acted against their best interest. I was concerned about the future of the planet.

In dairy production class we studied how to calculate the lifetime performance of dairy cows. To make it practical we were assigned to measure and weigh the food consumed by a cow and to record the lifetime output in calves and milk. When I returned with my findings the teacher told me that our cow had given birth to too many calves and that too much milk was produced with too high a fat content from the feed the cow had eaten. That made the production cost of our bio dynamic milk half of what regular milk was costing. This calculation did not include the savings on veterinarian services and antibiotics, which would have made the difference even greater. To make his opinion scientific, he asked me to bring samples of our hay and silage as well as ground meal the cow was fed during milking. The results came back from the lab with the remark that our hay contained herbs that had disappeared from the pasture land of this region with the use of nitrogen and phosphorus fertilizers when farmers began to spread them together with pelletized lime.

"Your hay is a rare diet mixture used for boosting health of highly valued racehorses. Such diet hay is only available from Swiss Alps at a very high price." I was told. He took my agriculture class on a field trip to inspect our "Pasture Museum" as he called it. We explained to the class that no artificial fertilizers or pesticides have ever been used on this farm.

"Lucky you," the teacher conceded. "Maybe you Bios are not that crazy after all."

Soon after this scientific excursion my apprenticeship was complete.

I participated in a statewide essay contest for students of technical and trade schools. I won the contest for my region. It had the title: "What the public knows about the environment."

The winners were invited to the State House and banquets were given by the governor of State. I was seated next to the Governor, the Minister of Agriculture and the Minister of Education at the head of the table. After congratulatory speeches, contestants were encouraged to ask questions as this was a rare opportunity for students and public officials to engage in conversation. My question was to the ministers of education and agriculture. I said:

"I have just finished my classroom work in farming. I was tested on my understanding of the contents of our textbooks. I could not help but notice that the books we were studying were written, published and donated by the chemical industry. The words Environment, Ecology, and Biodiversity are not used in these books. The word Water is only mentioned in the context of diluting poisons and cleaning equipment. Irrigation and precipitation were mentioned as technical issues. Waterways and bodies of water that could be affected by farming, were never mentioned. Production of food was presented as an industrial activity, including all animal husbandry. No public health mandate is mentioned in this literature. Here is my question to you:

How is this possible that future farmers, who will be in charge of our environment and our nutrition are not being educated in these topics? How can you let the chemical industry write the textbook on farming? Is there no conflict of interest?" Instead of giving an answer or repeating my question, he asked:

"Which school did you attend"? When I named my farming school and the district, the Minister of Agriculture who had taken my question, simply gave a knowing "ah" and sat down. No answer was a big answer to me. He was working for the Chemical Industry, not for the people or the farmers."

CHAPTER SIXTEEN

JOURNEYMAN YEARS

"Three years of training in Agriculture were completed. To celebrate, I went with friends on a drive from Strasbourg in southern Germany to Santiago de Compostela in the region of Galicia in Northwest Spain, following the ancient "Saint Jacobs Trail".

It is the pilgrimage, undertaken as an alternative to visiting the Holy Land of Palestine. What intrigued me was the fact that this journey was also an architectural journey. Through the centuries, pilgrims had left building stones. Gifts used for the construction of altars, chapels and churches in Romanesque and Gothic styles. These structures are witness to the devotion of pilgrims.

The trail took us to a small village in Galicia, an ancient area where the inhabitants still speak a Celtic dialect. Entering a village was only possible on foot. It sets the traveler back for centuries. The houses were built too close together for modern vehicles to enter. Walking downhill into such a narrow street, I looked through an open half-door into a stable, where I could see a young cow in birthing distress unable to deliver her calf unassisted. Not speaking the language, I signed to the old couple who lived in the same building, that I would like to offer my help. Showing them my calloused farm hands as proof that I was a real farmer, they agreed to let me try. One hour later I had delivered a large healthy bull calf to the relief and delight of the old couple. After washing up, they insisted to offer us some of their Portuguese sweet bread and sweet milk coffee. I loved the big toothless smile and the drop of a tear in the eyes of these old people. This was all the thanks I needed. Saving a life was a powerful experience. It made our pilgrimage complete. At the end of this day we reached our destination: Santiago de Compostela.

After one Year as a Journeyman Farmer I was drafted by the German government to serve an alternative to military service. I was being tested for an assignment to go to Chad in Central Africa to join a project drilling for water for irrigation and drinking water in villages and on farms under a program sponsored by the German Development Service. We were being selected not by interview but by observing groups of up to 12 applicants in round table conversations with no pre-set topics. Each group had an observer. At the end, they were satisfied that they knew the talent each participant had brought to the table. I was accepted for deployment. Unfortunately, terrorists had killed reporters in that country and the program was shut down.

To continue my education in Farming, I applied for a scholarship at a College in Sussex, England to study Soil Sciences. I assisted my Professor, since I had completed training with one of the foremost soil managers in organic farming during my first year of apprenticeship.

During this time at college, my friends and I decided that more widespread knowledge about farming, food production and land stewardship was required to achieve better policy decisions in Government. We felt it necessary to give research a more consumer-oriented goal, rather than a purely production oriented industrial mandate with no regard to nature and public health. To this end, we organized a series of seven-day conferences for university students, farm apprentices, farmers and agricultural researchers on organic farms.

During these conferences, participants did all the farm chores, giving the farmers a week off, so they could participate in these conferences and contribute from their rich experience in very meaningful and productive discussions. Besides doing the farmer's chores, participants were invited to volunteer in food preparation, bread baking and serving banquet style meals three times a day. Experienced farmers, journeymen and farm apprentices were shadowing university students and academics to make sure the daily farm tasks were performed correctly. To many of the participants, these conferences turned out to be a life altering experience. For the first time, many became aware of how far removed society is from the reality of food production, land management and water protection. I wrote the task lists and timetables for everything that needed to be done from four o'clock in the morning to eight o'clock at night. I never had trouble finding enthusiastic volunteers for each task. At the end of the week, a final banquet was prepared and served during which all participants had a chance to introduce themselves again and to speak about their expectations, experience and personal take away.

Soon requests began coming in for our little group to create a farm school with a focus on organic research, farm education and training to provide graduates with a certificate in Bio farm management. We were hoping to qualify students to farm and to perform land trust management. Management Skills were not well developed at that time in Bio farm training. Public farm schools were teaching mostly things one must avoid to protect the environment.

During the nineteen sixties and early seventies the back to the land movement was making enthusiastic volunteer labor available to farms and turning Bio farms into Eco-tourism destinations. This was causing economic stress on small organic farms. Questions about labor and social justice had to be addressed. Farmers were overwhelmed by volunteers who had to be housed, fed and trained. These activities took away from a farmer's time to attend to his work. Work done by inexperienced helpers did not always make up for this time. Farms needed help to reorganize and to meet these challenges.

Before the year at College was over, I was invited to consider taking over the management of a secluded 400+ acre farm in Bavaria with large unfinished buildings located in a valley bounded by gently rolling hills and forest land. The previous owner had intended to breed racehorses there. He had begun building stables, guest quarters, an industrial alcohol distillery and cattle-finishing stables for 80 bulls. He suddenly passed away. The farm was available for a new mission.

A Bio scientist called me to see if I was interested in supporting the creation of a research facility and farm school at this site. My job was to be the completion of the facility, to start up the alcohol distilling factory, to obtain the distilling license and to be the trainer, planner and manager of the farm operation with an apprenticeship program. Enthusiastically and with the help of friends I said yes and we jumped right in. We repaired and completed mechanical systems, completed the commercial alcohol still which was to serve as a source of funding for the research and training facility.

Before snowfall and frost in November, we plowed all the arable land. A friend and I ran the plow around the clock six hours on six hours off until we had the 400-acre spread done. I loved the smell of freshly turned earth. We finished the job and it began snowing while we were rinsing off the plow. We developed a 14-year crop rotation plan. After completing construction and testing of the distillery, we obtained the license to produce industrial alcohol. We had purchased the required livestock and made all systems operable. For organic fertilizer we were planning to produce composted liquid manure, using aeration in combination with biological composting ingredients and herbal enhancers to spray out on fields and plants. Our plan was to partner with other farms around the region to produce organic crops for the distillery. The waste of which would be fed to the bulls, producing organic beef.

We had been told that Lawyers were working on trust documents for our research foundation, which would assume ownership of the farm when suddenly we were informed that the property had been sold in a land swap. When we inquired what the meaning of this was, we were told that unfortunately the farm had to be traded for urban development land outside of the City and that there was nothing the owner could do about it. The scientist and his friends had managed to achieve a large financial gain in real estate value by licensing the distillery. The developer was now harvesting the results. He came personally to the farm to explain the change of plans. He offered a token amount of money as severance pay. I felt used and was furious. I told him to keep my severance pay.

"The commitment I made was priceless. I am not for sale." I felt sorry for all the participants. I walked away from this conversation with my head high and my dignity intact. Mira the pet pig who ran with my dogs peed on the tires of his golden Mercedes 600, because she had not been told that she was not a dog."

Now in my wounded state I was remembering this betrayal. I felt alone, helpless and useless. I wanted to end this uselessness. I was hit by another wave of flooding. I could not forgive myself for this failure. I had spent nine months without a proper contract on good faith. I now was profoundly tired.

"When word got out that I was I free, I was offered a management position at the farm to which I had apprenticed myself during my first year of training five Years earlier. This offer came with an option to purchase this property five Years hence. I felt good about this quick turn of events."

CHAPTER SEVENTEEN

YOU HAVE TIME

"Before starting this new project, I needed to take a break to get some distance and to clear my head. The experience in Bavaria had been a good one. We had run another farm conference there. It was well attended and successful. The conference was given a piglet by one of the participants to cook and serve as a meal. I was not surprised when the participants voted to give the piglet a name instead. They named her Mira. Mira ran with our two black Hungarian sheep dogs, Romulus and Remus. We gave Mira her own stall, next to our horse with whom she fell in love instantly, plucking clover outside to feed to him in his stall. The dogs moved in with Mira because here they found food. Mira had decided she preferred dog food. The dogs were now living on Mira's diet. Mira grew fast. She was just waiting for her voice to break, so she could bark like the dogs. Mira acted like a dog including raising her leg to pee. She could run as fast as the dogs. Local farmers were walking the fields on Sundays dropping a jaw when they encountered a rider on his horse and two black dogs with a strapping pink pig running as a threesome. Mira always in the lead. This trio was being talked about.

In the local farming community, I had established good relationships. Our next-door neighbors did not know what to make of us at first. They were very shy, refused to sell us produce from their gardens, milk, eggs or honey from their bees.

"We promised these things to someone already", they told us.

One night at two o'clock in the morning there was a knock at our door. The neighbor's son had come over to ask for my help. A first birth of one of their heifers had stalled. They had been unable to reach their veterinarian. They did not know what to do. They were afraid to lose the mother and the calf. I was the last resort.

"Go to your cow, place fresh straw next to her, bring a large bowl of hot water and a bar of soap. Cut two one-inch thick sticks of wood about a foot long and find two three-foot long pieces of rope plus the biggest bath towel you have. I will be right over. This is going to be a hard fight." When I arrived, the cow was panting exhausted from too many hours of labor.

"How long ago did the water break?" I asked.

"We don't know. We did not see it. When we came in to milk the cows she was in labor".

"I will need both of you to help ". I had them spread the fresh straw and hand me soap and hot water. I applied soap liberally to my arms. Then I lubricated the heifers birth canal. I reached in to turn the calf to make sure the navel cord was not wrapped around its neck. I asked them to attach a piece of rope to each of the sticks. The other end of the rope I fastened to the calf's front feet.

"All three of us have to do the work for this mother now. She is spent. Do exactly as I say. My hand will be inside guiding the calves' body. When I tell you, start pulling firmly but gently. We will pull out one foot, then the head, then the other Foot. This is a large calf. We will need to get the shoulder sideways. When the hip comes, we go sideways again. I will try not to tear anything. Back off when I tell you and have soap and water in reach in case I need more lubrication. When the calf comes out the amniotic sack might come out as well. We must clean it and push it back in before the cow gets up. After that we make sure she does not squeeze it out again with the afterbirth. Soak the towel in water for me." Fifty minutes later we had delivered a large, healthy bull calf. The amniotic sack had indeed come out. We cleaned it and placed it back inside. The calve started breathing, after I cleared the airway.

"Towel please," I stuck out my hand. I took the soaking wet towel, stood up tall and slapped it on the cow's back as hard as I could. The loud bang startled the exhausted mother. She jumped up onto her feet. Two minutes later she was licking her calf.

Two lives had been saved. From that day on I could have asked for anything on this farm. I had become part of this family.

My friend from college who had helped me with the farm project in Bavaria, lost her mother while we were busy setting up the farm. She was heartbroken when she realized that no one in her family had sent her the news until several months later. Her father was living on an Island near Boston, Massachusetts. I suggested that we should go visit her father and give her a chance to say goodbye to her mother.

"You can be my guide on a ten-week tour of the United States. I want to meet as many people as possible, to learn as much about America as I can. Why don't we make this a hitchhiking trip?"

We made up a sign that said Munich to LA. We left Munich by train to travel to Bonn where we were going to catch a charter flight to Kennedy Airport. As the train was descending from the Swabian Alb, it came to a sudden abrupt stop. It had crashed into a freight train sitting on our track at the railroad station at the bottom of the slope. Remarkably, the place where our railroad car came to a halt was exactly across from a monument honoring the engineer who had designed this very steep and difficult railroad passage. This engineer was a forbear of mine. Right now there was no time to linger or to reflect on genealogy. We had a charter flight to catch. Not getting to the airport would mean to forfeit the ticket. I suspected that there might only be one taxi at this small station. Without hesitation we ran down the hill and were first to reach the taxi stand. We got into the only cab and begged the driver to take us to Stuttgart Main station as fast as he could. Luckily, he agreed. We were on our way again. Once at the main station in

Stuttgart we were told that in order to get reimbursed for the taxi ride we had to go to Bahn Headquarters and talk to the chief of operations. The taxi driver took us to railroad headquarters. I literally jumped over the receptionist's desk when she tried to tell me that I did not have an appointment.

"I know," I replied. "We just came from the railroad collision and we had no appointment to crash our train either. Now we have a plain to catch in Bonn and a taxi to pay for. We will lose our tickets if we do not make this flight. Please help us?"

Once inside the administrator's office the director knew about the crash and acted calmly and promptly. He refunded our taxi, looked at the schedule for the next train to Bonn and handed us first class tickets for the Inter City. Unbelievably, we arrived at Bonn HBF one hour earlier than the scheduled arrival of the wrecked train. Acting without hesitation had done the trick.

Once in New York, we decided to hitchhike east. Travelling on Interstates, we switched rides at service plazas until we came to a harbor town where we found out that there was no passenger ferry to this island. We finally made it to the ferry terminal in time for the last boat.

The introduction to the Island was made by my companions father, who was living in a Victorian house. He gave us a whirlwind tour of the Island and introduced us to many people. We learned about the island towns and the Native population, while admiring the natural beauty of this place. We visited the grave site of her mother and paid our respects. This was very hard for my friend and her father. The community was still in mourning.

The parents had established a country store here. Everyone knew and liked the founders. Both her parents were seen as pillars of this community. The store was a gathering place first and a store second. It offered healthy foods and nutrition ideas, hand woven natural fabrics, Irish woolens and hand-woven silks and cottons. We received a heart warming welcome, but we had to move on.

Travelling across America was an eye-opening experience for me. The landscapes offered similarities to landscapes I had seen in Europe except for the size: Foolishly I found myself trying to compare even though there was no real match. The forests were bigger, the Interstate highway was sweeping in large generous curves cut through rock outcroppings of ancient mountains. I was able to observe small industrial towns with dormant factories next to rivers with little dams, serving hydropower generators. I was wondering what people were doing for a living now. As expected, drivers shared their stories and offered their opinions about the economy, the country and their lives. Some warned us about the people in the next State:

"It's ok here, but in the next State you can't trust people. Watch out." It was at times difficult for me to follow all that was said. My English was still dependent on good acoustics, which was hard to find with engine and wind noise in moving vehicles. For twelve hours a day I was witnessing amazing landscapes stream by like a great Imax presentation. America, live stream. I was overwhelmed, I was in awe and I fell in love with this amazing place. At times my travel companion accused me of not talking to her any more. I was simply not able to process all the information that was streaming in on me from all sides, seven days a week, twenty-four hours a day. New language, new people, new world, new thoughts. We were looking at all the same things, so verbalizing what we both had just seen seemed redundant to me. The sign we were holding up to hitch rides said: Munich to LA.

"Where is Munich?" people would ask. "In Pennsylvania?"

"No, it's in Germany near the Oktoberfest."

"I see" They would say. "Everyone had heard about that."

Once the Eastern mountains were behind us, the Lakes region and the great plains came into view. We decided to travel I 90 as far as Saint Louis Missouri, then west on route sixty-six. America took my breath away. I had never seen such space. Never had I seen such skies. Indiana was flooded from early summer rains. I could see farmers kayaking through their corn fields. Occasionally we were riding with families who were "doing the great journey" in their super equipped RVs with their children and their pets to see the parks and the sights before their children would be too old. They came equipped with self-propelled Camper trucks, a small four wheel drive vehicle in tow, a boat on top of the camper, a cross country dirt bike mounted above the trailer hitch, mountain bikes strapped to a rack in the back of the four-wheeler. This sparked my curiosity and I took a series of pictures of American travel gear. I also took pictures of the great plains, that show absolutely nothing. I wanted to show my friends back home how much of nothing there was here. (The Canadian Border Police later confiscated and destroyed all my films. They were searching for pot. Pulling my undeveloped films out of the reels was an act of malice. We had no pot.) At night we tucked ourselves behind bushes in our green king size tarp envelope into which we slipped our sleeping bags. Occasionally we went into towns to stay at a motel to do laundry, take showers and to stock up on food supplies. One of our drivers said:

"You think these great plains are something? Wait until you see the Grand Canyon. That is going to blow you away." The landscape now featured an ancient Ocean Floor with amazing rock outcroppings. We would have stopped for all of them but were still in the European habit of staying on schedule and the Grand Canyon was our next destination.

When we arrived at the south rim and I looked into the depth of this geological wonder, I was speechless. I decided to hike down the Kaibab Trail and up the Bright Angel trail. Being unfamiliar with this area, I consulted with a park ranger. He suggested I take no water and just a light snack, because I could buy food and water at the Phantom Ranch all the way down by the river. I began my descent down Kaibab Trail, which at the top started as an easy trail through scrub pine and shrubbery. Vistas into this huge canyon with its layers of sedimentary rock in a rich palette of colors took my breath away. On my way down I could feel the temperature rise on this cloudless day. There was no shade. I read:

"You are now entering a zone where temperatures can be comparable to a desert in Mexico, reaching in excess of 120' Fahrenheit. Now I remembered the advice of the ranger, not to bother carrying water. I had never been in such a hot dry place before. I was still taking pictures. I noticed the onset of dehydration. It became more and more difficult for me to walk, even down this steep trail. Soon I had to talk to each of my legs, commanding it to take one more step. Finally I reached the suspension bridge. None of the rock outcroppings along the trail had given me shelter or shade from the blazing sun. Mules and horses carrying visitors had used the available shade to rest and to relieve themselves. In my deteriorating condition I was unable to tolerate the odor. Now I found myself on a bridge right above the river. To my great disappointment it was still a very long way to the Phantom Ranch and the cool water of the Colorado River. After what felt like an eternity of struggle, I reached the river and walked right up to my neck into the water, hoping to lower my core temperature. After a while I attempted to drink from the water. My body rejected the liquid violently. Now I knew I was in trouble. I went to see the ranger at the Phantom Ranch, described my condition and asked for his advice.

The Ranger looked at me and said:

"You have heat stroke. And you are suffering from dehydration. First, we have to get some salt into you. After we have saline balance, you can sip and retain water. Then we will see about food. First, we must re-hydrate you. Take tiny sips of water. Here are five salt tablets. Swallow one each hour for the next five hours. Then come back and see me." I thanked him and found a shady place to rest. I dried my clothes and boots and began taking salt tablets. I started to feel better and I took very small sips of water from a bottle of water he had sold me.

While I was resting, I thought about my choices. By the time my salt intake was complete and I had eaten some food, it would be nine pm and pitch-black in the Canyon. I could stay the night here but that meant a similar experience climbing out the next day. One vertical mile up in this unforgiving heat with a body unadjusted to this climate. That was not an option. I told the ranger about my decision to begin walking up.

"There is another ranger station half way up Bright Angel Trail. You can rest there and finish the hike in the morning. A lot of hikers do that" the ranger told me.

A little after nine pm I began to walk up the trail, feeling with my feet the difference between the trodden trail and the rough beside it. Some distance into the trail, I was stunned by the silence that surrounded me like a holy place. The distant gurgling of the water was suddenly interrupted by footsteps ahead of me with a distinct clunking sound with every other step. I thought to myself:

Here I am, feeling sorry for myself while there is a person with an artificial leg struggling to walk up in the dark. When I caught up with the hiker, I found that it was a teenager who had gotten separated from his family earlier that day by running ahead down the Kaibab Trail. The noise I heard was not an artificial leg but came from a care-package, the ranger had sold him. The boy told me that he was from Houston, Texas and that he was not used to walking more than a few city blocks at a time. he was wearing city shoes. The dark had surprised him. Now he was unable to feel his toes, which he believed were bleeding from hitting rocks and stumbling over roots. He groaned every time his feet touched another obstacle. I told him I would stay with him as far as the bright Angel Ranger Station half way up. I took his pack and told him to hang on to my arm. At one-point several young park employees came running up the trail, carrying flash lights. I asked them, if I could have one of their flash lights to help this injured boy walk up the trail. They refused.

"This is our day off. We are out of here." With these words they were gone.

The boy was in serious pain. His whining had begun to take its toll on me. Finally, we arrived at the Bright Angel ranger station. His feet were done. I was done with him. He had stumbled over every rock and every root. He was in pain and exhausted. At the ranger station, many hikers were laying under trees in the grass, sleeping. Now the boy wanted to wake the ranger and order a helicopter to fly him out.

"I tell you what you will do" I told him "you will lay down here with the other hikers for the night. Like everyone else, you will get some sleep. Don't even think of waking anyone or the ranger. You are not an emergency. You will be fine." When he kept whining, I thought of knocking him cold for his own good, but I changed my mind. Instead I said:

"I will continue on up and find your parents. I expect them to be running back and forth between trailheads. They will be in panic by the time I find them. I will tell them where you are and that you are safe here. I will tell them to expect you up on the rim between eleven and twelve o'clock tomorrow. I will tell them to go to the lodge and catch some sleep. No. Don't thank me. Just lay down and don't wake anyone."

He did. I never saw him or heard from him again. It was pitch black. I had no idea what he looked like. I found his parents, who were worried sick and as exhausted as their son from running back and forth between trailheads just as I had expected. I told them that their boy was fine and to go to bed. It was now past three o'clock in the morning. A few years later I found a head cam video of both the descent down Kaibab Trail and the ascent of Bright Angel Trail. Now I knew that this night, my guardian Angels had been with me. I had unknowingly missed every opportunity to trip and fall off the edge of the trail or to step into the abyss at one of the many lookouts. Looking at these videos made my adrenaline kick in and my heart race.

Our Journey continued west. The generosity and hospitality we encountered were wonderful. I had never met nicer or friendlier people in my life. They came from all walks of life and from all four corners of the world. my limited English never got in the way of my understanding their circumstances, lifestyles and attitudes.

Our next destination was Beverly Hills where we attended a lecture on organic gardening and farming at a community college. Our soil science Professor from College in England was giving a lecture on humus development and soil fertility. He was delighted and surprised to see his assistant and one of his students here. Next stop was the Bio-garden at the University of Santa Cruz. The people there were interesting, "out of the box" thinkers and innovators. I was sorry I could not stop the world and get off right then and there, to join them in their work. We concluded the West coast loop by visiting San Francisco. We saw giant Sequoias, visited Yellowstone and Yosemite. We saw interesting places people were eager to show us from abandoned gold mines to tiny ski resorts and of course the blue Jewel of the West, stunning Lake Tahoe. On to Nevada, Humbold county and the great Salt Lake, Idaho, Wyoming, Colorado. Crossing from Detroit to Windsor, then east on Canada's route 1 above the Great Lakes to Ottawa and Montreal. We proceeded to Niagara Falls and on into Vermont, New Hampshire and finally back to the island where we had started.

What a fabulous trip! What a wonderful country, what gracious hosts. I felt gratitude to my travel guide who put up with me and my weird sense of humor. I was exhausted and had to rest for a few days before it was time for me to return to Europe.

Upon my return to the Island, a letter from my mother was waiting for me. She wrote that the farm which I had agreed to manage, beginning in the Fall, was no longer available. The farmer's oldest daughter had heard about my agreement with her father and decided to take my position herself. I remembered that my mentor and teacher had told me of his one life wish: That one day one of his children would take over his work. Now this wish had come true and I was glad for him, glad to have been the push for his oldest child to make his wish come true.

My mother's letter began with the words:

"Dear Sunny, you have time."

For the first time in my life, I had time. I was twenty-five Years old. I had only just scratched the surface of this amazing Continent. I have to admit I was in shock about the loss of a second farm project in a row. I had to go back to Germany to run another Bio-conference on a farm near Frankfurt. I was determined to come right back and to see what more I could learn about America. When I arrived at JFK Airport in New York to fly back to Germany the hall was full of German passengers searching for their charter flights. No one was able to locate their agent nor did we see an announcement about a cancellation or a relocation of our return flight. The charter outfit that brought all of us to the United States had vanished. Hundreds of People with charter tickets in their hands were stranded and understandably very upset.

I had no time to be upset. I had to get to Germany to run a conference. I had to travel today. I found one seat on a Lufthansa flight to Frankfurt, which was in the process of boarding. They understood my predicament. Lufthansa advanced my airfare to Germany and back to the USA.

The conference took place on a large farm with many activities including a Bio bakery, dairy, poultry, sheep, market gardens and direct marketing into Frankfurt. As all the previous conferences, this one was once again a great success. The participants felt better integrated and knowledgeable about the possibility of food production without poison."

I told my trauma counsellor:

"Even though I was returning to the United States after this conference, I will now recount the continuation and conclusion of my farming career, because the next event ended my engagement with farming and added a major betrayal to the list of my injuries.

The success of this latest conference prompted another invitation to me and my associates to take over management of a farm located in Austria.

The idea was once again to create a Bio farming school, partnered with a viable farm operation offering Bio management training and research, leading students to graduate with a certificate in organic farm management.

My assignment was to spend time on this farm and to evaluate its potential for this purpose. I agreed to spend nine months there and report my findings to my associates at the end a farm conference we were to organize on this estate.

The farm was presented to us as a well-established, self-supporting and profitable enterprise. It was located in a valley with gently rolling hills, small forested slopes and vegetated brooks separating fields and pasture land with a paved country road winding its way through the middle of the farm. The buildings were beautifully designed by Italian architects about a hundred years ago and was recently renovated. The dairy barn is a handsome structure with an alpine style second story drive through loft for hay wagons and a gabled roof with large flaring overhangs covering outdoor stables. Utility buildings are scattered over the farm yard like a small village with drives connecting them. One contained a grain mill another a root cellar with grain storage above. One was used as a bakery one housed a workshop and shelter for farm equipment and two small structures were housing pigs. All roofs are decked with red clay tiles. The walls are brushed with burnt yellow stucco often seen in Italian architecture. Across the road was a beautiful market garden with a large garden house. This building is an assembly hall with an open floor plan accommodating up to sixty people.

All this looked very promising to be a partner operation to go with farm education and research. Presently the farm had three apprentices. The herd consisted of thirty cows and twenty heifers. Calving season started a few days after I arrived. We delivered healthy calves and had them lined up in little stalls, when I received a telephone call from a veterinarian. He introduced himself and asked me if everything was alright.

"Why do you ask?", I wanted to know.

"You have not called me"

"Why should I call You?" I asked.

"For the last ten Years I have delivered all the calves on this farm, treated calves for diarrhea, gave cows antibiotics for udder infections and was called for medical emergencies on a regular basis."

"I did not know this," I said. "We have not had any medical emergencies since I came here. I took charge of the herd for the winter and I am training apprentices. Would you like to come by and see the herd? I would like to meet you and hear from you what you think of the herd now. It would be a social call, not a medical one, unless you see something we need to look at. I have some questions I would like to ask you."

"It would be my pleasure," he said.

The following day the veterinarian came by and looked at our calves.

"Wow", he exclaimed. "This is the best lineup of calves I have seen on this farm. No wonder you did not called me."

"Take a look at the rest of the herd" I invited him. We went around and inspected the livestock and talked about the merits of keeping a breeding bull vs. artificial insemination. He explained the lineage of various cows in this herd. He pointed to a heifer that showed promise to me and stated:

"Daughter of Sun. Best line here. Best in the valley

"How much do you charge for an average delivery?" I asked.

"$X00.to $X000.- depending on the time of day or night and up to $X0000.- or more, if there are complications."

"That is roughly $ XX.000 a year for the dairy alone. If you add visits to see calves and treat infections, it could be even more. No wonder you called. Is this your biggest account in the valley?"

Yes," he replied. "Until you showed up." We both laughed.

On a congratulatory note the veterinarian left me to my chores. The following week the owner had one of the apprentices stop what I had assigned him to do and ordered him to build a horse stall.

"I bought a horse for my son's birthday," he explained.

"What did it cost you?" I asked.

"Why, nothing," he said.

"The horse trader gave it to You?"

"No, I traded it for this heifer." He pointed at the animal the veterinarian had identified as the most valuable offspring in this herd and the best line in the valley.

"You did well" I said to him. To myself, I said:

"You just sold offspring from your best line for a piece of salami. You set the breeding program for your herd back ten years." I could not help it but to be very upset. As a farmer and as a breeder, this trade made me unhappy. I realized it was not my place to worry about the decisions of the owner. It put a cloud over our prospect of creating a farm school and research partnership, however.

At the shop our apprentices were taking farm machinery apart to replace broken parts and to lubricate moving parts. We were spray painting the finished machines with fresh green rust proofing paint complementing the farm logo. I took parts that needed replacing to the local farm equipment shop to order replacements.

"What is going on?" asked the mechanic. "What do you need these parts for?"

"Our machinery is in the shop for winter maintenance".

"What shop, and what do you mean by winter maintenance?" He said, laughing out loud. "They have never done any maintenance work on that farm! I did not know they had a shop" He exclaimed.

"Tell me then, what did they do?" I wanted to know.

111

"Normally, they leave the machines in the field and wait until they are needed again. Then they pull them out from where they were left. If they do not work, they send for us to come pick them up and to fix them here at our shop. Always an emergency. Always last minute. Always now, now, now." He repeated: "Nothing but emergencies. Then they use them and leave them until the next time around. What you are doing is not normal. What happened? Did they sell the place? Are you working for the new owner?"

"I am managing the farm this winter. With the help of our apprentices we do what farmers do. Get everything in working order, so we are prepared when the time comes." I stepped close to him. In a low voice I asked: "Tell me, how much bread am I taking off your table?" He mentioned a very large number.

"This Year we are doing it at the farm and I will appreciate it if you can supply these parts. I do not believe in emergencies. I am a trainer. I have to show our trainees how it's done.

"I know," he smiled a somewhat disappointed smile. I ran into more such expense accounts, I was beginning to be concerned about the viability of this farm for our purposes. I began to think that that we were called to save this farm. I began finding large amounts of money being spent all around the region, while work was being done inefficiently if it was not outsourced altogether. The foreman was spending weeks preparing long stacks of firewood.

"Are we selling firewood?" I asked.

"No, this is for the house." He replied. We have a very modern multi fuel furnace. It can burn every kind of fuel."

"How much time do you spend cutting and splitting wood and servicing this furnace?" I asked.

"All Winter except on Wednesdays when I make my delivery run."

Soon I had a picture of what this farm could or could not do. I joined the owner's wife for breakfast one Sunday morning. She placed coffee in front of me. She began:

"Now that you have spent a few months here, what do you think about our farm?" she asked.

"Do you want pleasant breakfast conversation or would you like the truth?"

"The truth," she demanded. "I want you to tell me what you think and what you have found out about our farm. I know You have been asking a lot of questions."

"That was my assignment. As you know, we were told that this farm is self-supporting. I saw the books. Your husband showed them to me."

"So, what do you think?"

"I think this farm has been supported financially from outside sources. Not from sales.

She began to cry. I felt uncomfortable to be in this position.

"I am sorry. I did not want to upset you. But the way things are done here is not supporting this farm. It is supporting a lifestyle. It is supporting the community, the veterinarian, the blacksmith. The various vendors, the seed supplier. Your customers, even. Every process from seed to harvest to market is too complicated and takes too much time. From where I sit, I cannot see how the product this farm is selling on the market can possibly support the way it is produced. Things that are done in-house on regular farms are being outsourced. The dairy is a good example. All the revenue went to the veterinarian. We just bought a pony and paid for it with the most promising heifer. Farms do not function that way. I can see that there was a lot of money invested here. There is nothing wrong with that. You have every right to do so. It is my job to find out if your farm can partner with a farm school. A school cannot subsidize a farm. It has to demonstrate that a farm is viable and can make a profit. That is what students must learn." She kept sobbing. I felt sorry for her. "I will have to decline the qualification of this farm for our project and recommend to my associates to look further. I think what your husband meant to tell us was that your farm is not in debt. And that is certainly a good thing. We are asked to create a school and to do research, that of course will have to be supported by endowments. The farm component has to be run as a viable commercial enterprise."

"You are right about everything," she said through her tears. "I came here eight years ago when we got married. I had an inheritance. We have used up eighty percent and I am not willing to spend another dime. The remainder is for my boys. I am glad you told me the truth. I am glad I told you my part of the story. You now know that you were right. What you will tell Your friends at the end of your conference?"

"The truth." I replied. "Until then I will continue to manage the crew and the dairy, get your equipment in shape and try not to waste your money. I trust that we will have frank discussions about possibilities with you and your husband and with our supporters. I have to tell you right now, your husband cannot be the manager of this farm. He will have to be on the board of directors of a non-profit foundation by your side. I am afraid that he will not agree to our proposals. He is a proprietor who thinks of his farm as his domain. That is his privilege.

Last Week I had a confrontation with him, after I caught one of your sons standing on the trailer hitch of a one-axle trailer, holding on to the driver's seat, while one of his apprentices had the gear disengaged, so that he could coast down the hill faster. I told your husband that while I was here on your farm, I would not tolerate children or anyone else to ride on farm equipment that was not properly designed for passengers. He disagreed with me, telling me that this was his son and not mine I was talking about. Therefore, he concluded, it was none of my business. I answered, that this was true. However, I told him, if anything happens to one of your children or to anyone else on this farm, getting hurt because of safety violations, this victim would become my child too. I told him that this was not a point of discussion or argument. If he did not stop this practice of safety violations or if I should find any of his children, his employees or his guests riding on farm equipment and ignoring safety rules, I would go to my room, take my things and leave. No one was seen riding on farm vehicles since and I am still here to hold the farm conference as planned."

The conference took place. After the last session I was asked to give my report to the full assembly. When I announced that the farm was not able to sustain itself as the basis for a partnership with a Bio farm school and research facility, I was accused of lying and asked to leave by friends of the owner and a furious and disappointed assembly. Most of my friends and collaborators were present. Not a single person stood up in my defense or support, including my best friends and my own father. I was asked to leave the room. I was excluded from all further discussions. The owner's wife who had verified the truth about my observations and who's money had been invested, was not present. I had donated nine months of my time and paid for my own airfare to come here to do this. It was to be my last attempt of helping to create a farm school. I promised myself never to set foot on someone else's land again."

Chapter Eighteen

GOODBYE EUROPE
HELLO AMERICA

The farmer's older brother was living next door. We had become friends over the past few months. Now I stumbled into his living room in shock and disbelief. I told him what had just happened. He invited me to come to his house and to stay in his guest room.

"This happened to me also." He said. "I was disinherited. I became an inventor and entrepreneur instead. I have designed my own cultivating system for nurseries from seed to marketing. I sell 20 million plants every year.I lease the very best farmland. Now I am planning to market my inventions. I am finally able to finance my expansion into manufacturing."

He asked me to photograph and film his nursery cultivating system. Also, to document the testing of his newly designed hydraulic planting machine for a catalogue he was designing. He also asked me to translate his catalogue into English. He was scheduled to demonstrate this Planting machine in Bordeaux, France and asked me to film the event and to be his assistant during the field demonstrations. This was a good diversion from my present devastation. I had a few weeks' time before my scheduled return flight to the USA.

While I was busy with camera work and translations, he invited me and a friend to take weekend trips on his sailboat on the Adriatic Sea. He let us choose destinations. When it was my turn to pick a destination, I asked to sail to Venice, Italy. The sailboat was a very comfortable 36' cruising ship made in England with sleeping quarters aft and a small cabin forward in the bow, a well-appointed galley in the middle that could be converted to sleeping quarters at night. Approaching Venice under sail, we were able to stay under sail all the way to the Piazza San Marco, dropping sails at the very last moment. I felt like an ancient mariner arriving in the center of a trade route that connected the known world a long time ago. What an amazing experience! We spent the night across the canal from San Marco in a tiny harbor. From here we visited the town by taxi boats. We left the gondolas to the lovers. We were interested in the manufacture of hand made glass objects. We were delighted with the food, the ambiance, the wine and the people strolling in their best italian designer attire. No way to get further away faster in space and time than to sail to Venice and to stay the night on board a ship.

To do the planting machine demonstrations in Bordeaux, we traveled by car from Austria to Bordeaux, France. To make the journey more dramatic, we crossed back and forth over passes across the Spine of the Alps, gaining magnificent vistas of the Austrian, German, Swiss and French Alps. We saw river valleys, lakes, glaciers and snow-covered peaks. In all kinds of light with the haze and mist creating amazing silhouettes and stacked slopes and ridges only seen in paintings.

Once in Bordeaux, we were met by the host of this event. He told us about his work.

"I sell things" he explained. "Anything from Mirage fighter jets to barges full of wheat or boatloads of timber. I am a diplomat facilitating trade between Countries. Take Spain and the Soviet Union for example.

The Soviets do not trade with fascist Spain. That is where I come in. I buy Oranges from Spain. I purchase timber from Russia. From France I sell Oranges to Russia and timber to Spain. I de-politicize the goods. I do well and have passports for as many countries, as I trade with."

During our field demonstrations, we planted hundreds of plants into a gravel road in just minutes, impressing the visitors who were interested in this technology.

To celebrate the event, the Mayor of Bordeaux invited traders, manufacturers and vendors to the best restaurant of Bordeaux. His own. Bordeaux at its finest culinary show. After completing film shoot and camera work, I returned to the USA, grateful for the hospitality, generosity and friendship I had received.

The Island was beckoning. Through my family I told my friends that I was resigning from the farm initiative. The Island presented a perfect combination of a community of interesting people and close proximity to Boston and New York. Many families have lived here whaling, fishing and farming for a long time. There were families in the service industries, from first responders, hospital staff, shipwrights to home builders. There was a day tourist industry. There were family compounds, owned by a sampling of successful American businessmen, politicians, scholars, writers, painters, musicians and poets. I liked it. It intrigued me, it challenged me. I decided to live here. The warm welcome- back, hugs from people I met during my first short visit made me feel good. I was grateful for this generous reception. I was once again getting ready to reinvent my life. The past was now fading. New challenges and windows of opportunity opened up for me. Everything I learned so far, I could use here constructively. New skills needed to be acquired for the creation of a new life. I was looking to the past as having been a series of pre-qualifying exercises. Learning the English language was a priority. New activities had their own language and vocabulary. People were generous and helpful. Learning skills to serve the local economy and to make a living was my new project. Finding mentors to guide my next steps and to teach me about the way things are done this side of the Atlantic was key. I was lucky to find the very best instructors I could hope for."

Now in my flood of memories the betrayal by my friends and the failure of my plans in Europe are ripping through me. My sense of loneliness and my inability to share my feelings with anyone are compounded by my fatigue from lack of sleep and this flood of memories is crushing me. I am left by the side of the road crying.

"I have always been able to count on one thing. I am a lucky person. My reliance and unshakable faith in the goodness of people, my belief that everything has a price and that it is better to try a little harder, to pay a little more up front, would have to show positive results. This became true for me on the Island. The local bank president told me about his observations:

"I have been watching you get on your thrift shop bicycle early every morning, clad in your navy pea coat, riding off to work. I saw you working early and late at the store two doors down from our bank. I saw you ride off to your construction job in between. It has taken you two days to find work. Most people here take months to get work. I will explain to you how money is used, how accounts are opened, how credit works and how to formulate offers when you want to purchase a business or a home. You are a good credit risk for our bank. My office is open for you anytime."

There was much for me to learn. I was given the opportunity to become part owner of this food store. My decision to learn how to build wooden New England houses was aided by my love of architecture. For my training I found talented woodworkers, shipwrights and carpenters, willing to share their knowledge. An impressive talent pool, that can answer impossible challenges with constructive problem-solving skills and craftsmanship. These builders are able to erect wooden structures capable of withstanding hurricanes on land and at sea. My luck was aided by two things. I have a habit of being prepared and showing up when I am needed. Learning how to play a musical instrument has taught me that once a skill is acquired, I can own it and use it over and over.

One of my mentors invited me to join a group of craftsmen who were enjoying a daily coffee hour after work at a round table in front of a fireplace at a waterfront restaurant. After a few visits, I realized that I was in the company of exceptionally talented woodworkers. I made every effort to understand and absorb as many of the ideas that were being discussed as possible. This was my college of constructive problem solving. Even though I was just beginning to learn the language of construction, much of what I heard at this table would stay with me and come up in my mind years later, when it was my turn to solve impossible problems of my own and to find creative solutions myself. My most important mentor was a co-worker who taught me tirelessly the carpenter's construction language. The secret about things that had one name but were not exactly that, like lumber dimensions, nail sizes and the names of tools. A blessing was my foreman, a shipwright who demanded exact cuts every time, regardless of the purpose of the piece being cut. Repeating the same movement, the exact same way was something I had learned in music. This made me a very good cutter. I could always get my job back, even though my retail business demanded of me seasonal work interruptions from carpentry during each ninety-day summer season.

My retail business provided me with the opportunity to travel to New York City and Boston to buy goods for the Season. Owning a business on main street was a great way to grow into my new community. One day I asked my landlord, why the town was in mourning.

Why do you ask?" he inquired.

"I see evergreens in all your flower beds and planters everywhere in town. Where I come from, this means that a local dignitary has passed away. The town is in mourning."

"Oh no" he replied, laughing. "People die all the time. Evergreens are the only thing we can plant here, because of vandalism. If we plant flowers, kids rip them out as fast as we plant them."

"I have two flower boxes at my store. Would you mind if I planted geraniums?"

"Be my guest," he said, smiling slyly. "But I can tell you, they will be gone the next morning."

"I will buy a second set of plants so I can replant. I will make a pledge to you. I will keep replanting until the vandals have green hands and it gets to be a job ripping out my geraniums. I will file no complaints with the police. Let's see what happens." He laughed at my foolishness. The first night after I planted my geraniums was just like he had said. All my plants were strewn all over main street. The replacements I had in store, were quickly planted. By the end of the second week, only one plant was missing and by the end of the following week I had reached my goal. All my geraniums were left untouched. Soon thereafter I noticed, that more flowers were being planted around town. I was surprised when I was recognized by the local garden club "for making the town a more beautiful place to live, to grow and to play." I felt honored. This was a caring community and people were paying attention. To further combat vandalism, which I deemed to be an ownership problem, I suggested to my fellow business owners, to hand over the town to the grade and middle schoolers during the upcoming Christmas Season.

We turned our store windows over to the children and gave them permission to decorate them inside or outside any way they wanted. The result was that we could hear the words "my store, my window, my town" during this entire holiday season. The following Year vandalism was down by 60% according to the chief of police. Our kids said that this was their town now.

A special experience for me was the chance to serve on the traffic planning committee for three Years. I learned that to plan the future makes you responsible for it. Now people blame you for everything that happens. Reacting to predicaments, on the other hand, can make you a hero.

I played my French horn in our local orchestra and in stage orchestras for musicals set in scene by the High School and other theatre groups. I played music for church services and special occasions. Having a country store that sells fabrics, I was able to support the Children's Theatre and other theatrical initiatives with fabric remnants for their costumes.

Highlight at Christmas was my appearance as Santa Claus, greeting children to everyone's delight with my German Accent. Is that why people think good things come from Germany? These activities and my carpentry training, during which I read a book about building construction along with every project I worked on, made my first five Years in America fly by.

I was able to buy a waterfront home with guidance from my banking mentor. I had promised to consult with him about major financial decisions. I had almost forgotten but I called him at the last minute.

"I did not even discuss price with the owner," I told the banker.

"Why don't you tell him what you can do instead of telling him what his property is worth. That way he can think about what might work for him instead of arguing with you about the value."

"What can I do?

"I know the property. The bank can give you a first mortgage for x amount. You have y in cash. You ask the owner for a second mortgage of z to be paid off in full after five years, meanwhile paying interest only. Your offer is x+y+z. = xyz. I called the owner back that evening. I told him that I was not telling him what his property was worth but that I wanted to let him know what I could do. He listened to my proposal then immediately answered:

"Sounds ok to me"

"I beg your pardon?"

"Sounds good to me." he repeated. With my mentor's help I had now bought a waterfront home with five thousand dollars down. Everything was on the up and up until one day some people came into the store, who seemed very interested and nice. They copied our business and opened a similar store up the street from us. They offered the same line of goods, but priced them below wholesale. Our customers left. We were being forced out of business. We tried sidestepping for a while, by adding specialty foods to our offering. They did too. We put our business up for sale. I had reached the top pay for an employed carpenter and the cost of living increases had outpaced my earnings."

Now this memory was demolishing my self-esteem in a very profound way. Just like the collision that ended my life as it was known, the failure of our business was forced on me with similar speed and impact. I felt that I had demonstrated an inability to react in time. Guilt shame and self-blame were knocking me down now.

CHAPTER NINETEEN

MANHATTAN, THE OTHER ISLAND

"I had to find an alternative fast. A call came with a proposal in New York City. It was a chance to get involved in designing, building and running a store and restaurant. Here my people skills, construction experience, design skills and patience would be helpful. I jumped at the opportunity. This made Manhattan my other island. I was thirty years old and for the second time in America, I had time. Even though I did miss my engagement in the island community, I was looking forward to getting busy with my new discovery: New York City. I had reached the top of the pay scale on Island and only owning my own construction business would take me to the next level. The island retail business was winding down and New York City was opening its doors for me.

There was a storefront, which my friends pointed out to me. They had been interested to rent it to create a restaurant and a produce specialty shop. Owning a vegetable wholesale business and a small retail shop at the lower east side, they could supply this new venture directly from the New York wholesale market at Hunts Point with fresh produce and fruit daily. They were disappointed about not even getting an appointment with a leasing agent. I offered to give it a shot, to see the realtor and to speak to the listing agent. The following day I sat at the realtor's office for eight hours waiting for a brief moment of the agent's attention. At the end of the day they realized that I was not going away. I was able to get the agent to set up a meeting with the commercial property's manager in charge of this building. The storefront is in a beautiful turn of the Century stone building with commercial storefronts at the street level. Originally built as a hotel it now was restored and repurposed as a high-quality residential condominium building. The storefronts on the street level are facing a street connecting Washington Square in the south to Fourteenth Street to the North with Fifth Avenue to the West and Broadway to the East.

My conversation with the property manager began with a question: "Where are you from?"

"The Island."

"Then we are neighbors," he beamed. "My wife is running a Bed and Breakfast there."

We spoke in detail about my experience and our plans. We came to an agreement for a ten-year lease for these premises. I had my first impression about the pace of New York City. Within forty-eight hours a corporation was formed, papers were signed and we had a key to the desired storefront. Working around the clock, I built a produce and specialty food shop on the street level with a restaurant at the lower level. An existing set of winding stairs, dating back to the turn of the century, was leading down into what used to be a lobby. The floors were made of marble inlay and polished terrazzo. Downstairs, towards the street, exposed brick arches gave the space a feel of a cloister. We added backlit, antique stained glass windows to brighten it up.

While construction was underway, I began to inquire about services available in this location. Having been there day and night for a few days, I had observed that different storefronts were getting trash pickup services from different disposal companies. To tie our business into existing relationships and to respect territories and rules, I asked one trash hauler about our store front:

"Who picks up at number XX"? I asked the driver.

"That is not mine. It belongs to Dump."

"Do you have their phone number?

"Yes". He looked up the number in his little book.

"Write it down," he said." It is 212 555 1212."

"What is your name? I want to tell them who referred me when I call."

Pauli, tell her Pauli says hello."

"Thanks, Pauli, I am Sunny. I'll see you around." Then I called Dump.

"Hi I am calling about pick up service for number XX at University. Pauli from Trash Corps told me to call you. He told me to say hello. We are building a produce shop and restaurant here. We will need a four-yard dumpster. Can you service our account?"

"Sure can, your Dumpster will be around the corner on XX."

"Thank you." I gave her the usual information for a new account. What was your name again?"

"Jane."

"Thank you, Jane, oh and while I have you on the phone, do you know someone who can supply us with dairy products?"

"Sure thing, call Jack from Happy cow shack at 212 666 1313. Tell him Jane from Dump corps told you to call."

In this manner I assembled a list of vendors, who knew one another from the trash hauler to the dairy vendor, the egg person, the banana man, the baker, who made the most wonderful Italian desserts and cannoli to die for and who would also supply us with fresh dinner rolls every day. Most other goods were supplied by my partners, who were sending tirelessly everything I needed to construct the store and the restaurant, including their plumber, gas fitter and electrician. I had a chance to establish good working relationships with several lumber yards and building material suppliers. Invaluable was my collaboration with Paco, owner of Puerto Maintenance, who operated a business out of a lower level boiler room shop on the lower East Side. He seemed to know everyone, was well liked and catered to minority businesses downtown, midtown and uptown. Paco was most knowledgeable about all restaurant related installations and regulations. He could fix and install mechanicals and stood by his clients with advice and service around the clock. He was an important advisor to me. In Manhattan the clock is always running. We worked relentlessly and were open for business after twenty-seven days. During this time, I became friendly with the owner of a pub across the street, where I could sit at the bar, look at my storefront and think. As it turned out, this was a famous jazz club that was frequented regularly by world class jazz musicians, who played here and even came over to hang out to meet their peers late at night after performing at the Newport Jazz Festival. They improvised together for old time's sake after hours. I was permitted to stay on and listen. The owner knew how much I loved this music. I met musicians who I had no idea were still alive. I learned that this pub had supported Jazz musicians for many decades, giving them open mike and performance space no matter what the fashion of the day happened to be. This made his pub the home for generations of the most talented and famous jazz musicians.

One night, I looked out of the pub window when I saw someone getting ready to smash our store window with a brick. We had just finished a gold leaf design with our logo on it. I quickly walked across the street and said:

"Excuse me, but you may not want to do this."

"Why the fuck not?" I had no idea what to say next.

"My wife," I improvised.

"What about your wife?"

"If you make as much as one scratch on this window, she will find you. And when she does, she will make you feel sorry you were ever born. Better think about that." It worked. I had not moved an inch back while I spoke while he was holding his brick in a threatening gesture.

"Ok I guess," he said after three seconds, handed me the brick, turned around and left. I took the brick around the corner and put it into our dumpster. I Never saw him again.

"What was that?", the bartender asked when I returned to the pub.

"Nothing. The punk wanted to put a brick through our new window. I told him about my wife. I said she would get mad if he broke the glass and make him sorry, if he did."

"You have a wife?"

"I have one as far as he is concerned. He did not want an angry woman to mess with him." Everyone laughed.

I helped to develop the menu: Salads, soups, quiches, omelets, desserts and daily chef's specials. The store upstairs was our pantry where we were able to pick our ingredients when they were perfect. The base salad, with up to ten different leaves and pretty garnishes, the fruit salad, freshly cut, our quiches and desserts were received by our clientele with as much enthusiasm as our soups. Our dressings were original and good enough to be bottled and sold. The speed at which we were able to serve our meals was key. Manhattan people are always on the run. Waiting around is not an option. We were able to serve lunch faster than a fast food restaurant but used superior ingredients.

In the process of constructing the shop I became friendly with the building's supervisor, who showed me a basement room adjacent to our restaurant. He said that there was no use for this space.

"We could incorporate this room into our restaurant by creating an archway" I suggested. He asked the owner's for permission. For a small additional fee, we were able to double our seating capacity. Following trends in the City, the restaurant went through a number of transformations which were exciting and interesting. First was to drop the produce store and serve frozen margaritas in a Mexican fiesta atmosphere. Overnight, the space was transformed into a Mexican Fiesta. When the frozen margarita craze was over, a bar and a mezzanine were added at the street level. We installed monitors across the inside of the store window and created a video bar we called "SOUNDS" with a powerful sound system. To make this possible in a building with upscale condo apartments above, I had to build a suspended sound-proofed ceiling capable of intercepting any and all sound. This bar was beautiful and exciting but hard to manage with cooks and wait staff from the theater scene. Too much drama. The search was on for a calm, more predictable business model. Finally, Sounds was transformed into a Japanese restaurant and everything calmed down. My partners were Japanese. I am not made to watch restaurant staff do the same thing day in and day out. I am a builder. I cannot do repetitive work. I need new challenges. I like to construct habitat. I work to accommodate people's special needs and preferences. That gives me joy. Therefore, I resigned from the restaurant business and went back to work, doing alterations and renovations in the City."

Now in Maine, under the cloud of PTSD the ending of my engagement in the restaurant business in Manhattan felt like another failure and proof that no matter how hard I worked, no matter how hard I tried I could not make anything stick. I was doomed. PTSD was putting a gray filter on all my memories. Desperate, lonely, useless, trapped, no way out but one.

"What else did you do in Manhattan?" my counsellor asked.

"I handed my share of this business back to my partners and returned to construction. I enjoyed altering and renovating buildings. I was hired by the owners of the building, where I had built the restaurant in its various incarnations, as a construction supervisor. I was curious about real estate and property ownership, so I completed the NYU Real Estate Certificate Program, earned a Property Management Certificate at the Institute for Real Estate Management and worked as a partner with the PRX maintenance corp, that had helped me build the mechanicals of the restaurant.

Maintaining Manhattan is an undertaking unmatched anywhere in the world. It is a bedroom community for eight million people at night that swells to twelve million individuals during the daytime. Everyone needs water, food, sanitation, transportation and communication plus every form of personal care from exercise studios to hospitals. Add fire, ambulance, police and special security services and it is a phenomenal achievement to get through one day, never mind three hundred sixty-five days a year and as many nights." I took a deep breath. Finding the secret of how Manhattan is possible, what makes it work day in and day out twenty-four hours was my new quest. I found myself immersed in this relentless never-ending flow of activities".

"You mentioned your father and his visit to New York. How did this go?" Asked my counsellor.

"It never happened. He had a heart condition. During the time he wanted to come, it was too hot. Manhattan was having brownouts." I thought about his visit some more.

"I found him there. But not the way I expected. He never came personally."

"How was that?"

"One day I came out of a movie theater and felt chilled. Touching my chest, I realized that I was soaking wet. I became aware that this film is about a boy who was trying to find his dad. It touched me in a very deep place. It had made me shed tears in a constant stream for the duration of the film. Determined to find out what this huge reaction was all about, I went to see a psychiatrist for a consultation. I recounted the story about the boy and his dad. The boy's father had gone away on a train and never returned. Hearing about the search for the father, the therapist said:

"This is about your relationship with your father. We can start there. Tell me everything about him." For the next few sessions I told him what I remembered and what I was told about my early childhood. There were stories about my attempt to reach the train, the taming of the wild boy, accusations of disobedience, of being a "runaway" and my memory of beatings I had received for disobedience which were completely out of proportion to my offences. Searching for a more recent interaction with my father I recalled a letter I had received which had been both bewildering and devastating to me. In this letter he accused me of betraying him by giving up the important causes we were pursuing with teaching agriculture on farms. In this letter my father mentioned my projects as though they were his own. He was present when no one stood up for me and I was dismissed from my last project by the full assembly of my friends and supporters, including him. He mentioned the disappointment he felt. In his eyes I was abandoning his causes when I decided to give up my quest for farming.

"Especially now," my father wrote, "that I am coming to the end of my life and am going to die soon." This was devastating to me and very confusing. I never answered this letter. I had no idea what to say. I tried to ignore it." The therapist suggested that my father might have had a condition known as projective identity disorder". He described it as the inability of a person to differentiate between their own identity and that of another.

"Actions, intentions, successes and failures of another onto whom this identity is projected are experienced as if they were their own. We can start by creating the separation of you and your father." He reminded me that I was in charge of living my life. More than that. I did not only have the right, but a responsibility to live my own life. He said that I had an obligation to learn to live my life for myself and not for my father or anyone else. I had to learn to put myself into the center of my own life. I had to give up the obligation to be another's care taker. To see another's life as my mission.

"Your own life is your only mission." The psychiatrist had said.

"I don't know how to do this," I exclaimed.

"You will have to let him go. You will have to let him die just as he told you he would." My therapist continued: "You will mourn him, be angry with him, and go through all the emotions one feels after the loss of a loved one until you have reached a point where you can first forgive yourself and then him".

"I will need your help," I said.

"We must examine your father's condition some more. We might find some answers which will make this easier," he added. After listening to further episodes of my family life and descriptions of my father's interactions with our mother and his nine other children, the therapist concluded that my father had indeed a classic case of projective identity disorder.

"He did not return from the war whole. That is why you could not stop trying to find him. Part of him never came back." The following months were spent building my new self-assurance and enjoyment of life on my own terms without the burden of a superimposed purpose, reason to exist or the task to rescue the world or others.

"What about the search in the movie and my reaction?" I finally asked. "I was accused of being a runaway. I was severely punished for that".

"Remember the episodes at the beginning of your story, when you tried to board the train? You were risking your life trying to find your Dad and like the boy in the movie, you too have been trying to find your dad down the railroad tracks to bring him home to your family. Both not knowing where the tracks would lead. Like the boy in the movie, you too have never found your Dad. Like the boy in the movie you are still looking for him. This explains your big reaction to this boy's story. It is your story too. Now it is your job to live your life. When you are done grieving your father's death, you will learn to forgive yourself for not finding him. Then you can forgive him for projecting his life onto yours. You will eventually find him in your memory and in your heart the way you have always loved him."

"What was it about Manhattan that fascinated you?" My counselor in Maine asked.

"Life in Manhattan as a construction supervisor was my gateway into the inner workings of this beast of a City. Maybe it was also a way for me to find access into the inner workings of myself. One day I went to see a movie after work at a movie-theater two doors down from our construction site. It was a bitterly cold night. When I came out, white smoke was billowing out of the ground floor of the building I was constructing. I had left two hours earlier. Sirens and horns of fire engines were sounding a cacophony. Ladders were beginning to be deployed, hoses were being rolled out.

I walked into the mayhem and found the fire chief.

"I am the construction supervisor on this project. There is no fire." I told him. "It is all steam. They turned on the furnace today. There is something wrong with the high-pressure valve. Send me with one of your men with a strong flashlight, I show him the boiler room and we can shut off the furnace and the water."

"Who are you?" The chief barked.

"I am Sunny, the construction supervisor on this job, I work for Blackrose construction." He agreed to my plan. We saved the building from getting flooded in an attempt to put out steam with water.

"How did you stay so calm?" the fire chief asked.

"I have no idea," I replied. "Maybe growing up with nine spirited siblings at home helped? We had one disaster happening every two minutes when I grew up." At the same site, while making my daily rounds I walked into an apartment one day. I heard noises that did not sound like hanging sheetrock. When I entered the room, I found two men going at each other with steel pipes.

"Whoa," I called out. "What the fuck is going on here?" Both started talking at the same time. I stopped them. I asked them to start at the beginning.

"He owes me money," one said.

"What for?" I asked.

"A jacket." The man said.

"And you want to beat it out of him with a steel pipe?" I demanded. "I tell you what: You tell me how much he owes you and I will give you the money. How much?"

"Twenty-five bucks". I took out the money and handed it to him.

"I will have no blood on my job. If you have a problem, come see me. We'll talk. Now hand me these pipes." They handed me the pipes.

"You ok now?" Grunts. After returning to the office, I wrote my incident report. After reading it, my supervisor said:

"Sunny, if I ever see such an idiotic story from you again, I will fire You. Don't you know, this is about much more than money. These guys have an issue bigger than that. It is their sick sense of pride. They are too stupid to deal with it. That is why they use steel pipes. You are lucky they did not both turn on you. You are lucky they had no guns. This was about honor. Neither you nor I will ever understand them. Next time you let them go ahead and kill each other. Never step in. Not ever." He got a little more worked up." The other day a guy shows up during lunch break in apartment six eleven and offers the men a sheetrock gun for twenty bucks.

"We don't need one," they said. Turns out the schmuck had just stolen this gun from apartment six fourteen and was trying to sell it to the guy he had stolen it from. A day later we heard of a similar incident on another job. A body was found at the bottom of an air shaft. Word was, he tried the same trick but got caught, because someone recognized the tool. They walked him to the air shaft opening and let him go. Nobody knew from nothing. They are crazy. Never mess with crazies. Promise?"

"Promise". I replied. This man was coach and mentor for me.

Weeks later on a very rainy day I set out to go to the seventh avenue subway down a pedestrian tunnel, to cross from sixth to seventh avenue. My wandering thoughts were interrupted by the point of a knife appearing under the rim of my rain hat and I heard something like:

"Wallet, money and honky mother fucker". My reaction was instant and explosive. My brain went into a state and time began to appear in slow motion.

"Spin", my brain said. "The chin", it said. "With the back of your fist", it said. "Wait for the head to come down", it said. "Now kick it like a soccer ball" it said. The back hand under the jaw disabled the attacker. My steel towed construction boot finished this confrontation. The whole thing took only a split second. I walked to the end of the tunnel. My hand started hurting and my ankle reminded me that something had just happened. I turned around to look and sure enough something dark was laying in the middle of the tunnel on the concrete floor. I continued walking down the stairs to the subway platform. The uptown train pulled into the station. When I sat down my knees started shaking violently.

Breathe, breathe, breathe. I said to myself. By the time I arrived at ninetieth Street and Broadway I had calmed down. I was able to speak about the incident with my colleague at the construction office. He opened his desk drawer.

"That is why I have this". He said. "It is loaded and security is off."
He cautioned me: "Never take out a gun unless you are prepared to
use It".

Another friend took me to a gun range. I shot with each hand. One
clip each. I made one hole in each of the targets. Six bullets each at fifty
feet. My friend brought up the target.

"Are you sure this is the first time you have fired a gun? You are a
great shot we need you on our team".

"I am sure you do. My expertise is with a home-made slingshot. I
think I will stick with that. do you have a slingshot range with slingshot
competitions?"

"I know you are a conscientious objector. Was gunplay a problem
for you in Manhattan?" My therapist asked.

"It was mostly removed from where I was standing even though
I knew as many people who did get shot, killed or hurt by guns in
Manhattan as people on the Island who came to harm in single car
accidents by going out of control, drunk or sober. I was more puzzled
by the culture of violence in Manhattan."

"What do you mean?"

"One Friday afternoon at my friend's business office one of his
employees stormed in.

"I am going to kill her", he shouted.

What's going on?" My friend inquired quietly.

"She is cheating on me!" He shouted. "I need a gun".

"Ok" said the boss and calmly took out a gun from his desk drawer
and handed it to his worker. The man spun around to storm off with
the gun in his hand. "Didn't you forget something?" My friend called
after him. Stopping himself with the door in his hand the man asked:
"What."

"Ammo. The gun is empty," his boss explained. He reached into
the drawer again and counted out a clip full of bullets. As he handed
them to the young man he said:" Are you sure you want to do this? If
you run off halfcocked like this, you will be a very dead Puerto Rican
before the day is over". We met for lunch at a Deli a few days later. I

had joined his service company as a partner to oversee carpentry, write proposals and work orders.

"What happened with the killing Spree?" I asked.

"He came back the next morning. I smelled the gun. It had not been fired. He returned all the bullets."

"She is not worth it," he told me. "I thought about it. She is not worth a single bullet."

The owner of the Deli came over to greet us.

"Hello guys. Have anything you want, it's on the house," he said.

After we had been served my friend asked me:

"So how much was your sandwich?"

Why it was free," I said. "On the house."

"U-Uh" he sounded. "This, my friend, was the most expensive sandwich you will ever eat."

Not two weeks later at two o'clock in the morning, I received an emergency call from the Deli, begging me to please come and remove a stoppage in the dish wash system.

"The whole storage area is getting flooded. We will have to close the place down," The voice yelled excitedly.

"Give me twenty minutes". In the middle of the night I found myself doing the backstroke in a twelve-inch-deep pool of dirty dish water in a small space beneath the dishwashing system, cleaning out a grease trap and removing the stoppage with my bare hands.

But the sandwich was delicious. I heard myself chuckle to myself.

I had found one of the answers to the question how Manhattan works: When push comes to shove, people in New York City will be available to help each other, no questions asked.

"The City never sleeps" is true. The word 'No' is not easily used if one can say 'Yes'. The worse it gets the more they stand by each other. They pay it forward into the favor bank.

The owner of an Asian restaurant approached me to see if I could make him an offer to replace the wooden strip oak floor in his dining room. I asked how much time I had. He said that the last customers were usually done by nine pm and that the staff would want to set up the dining room again at six o'clock in the morning. I told him that I would have to make a few calls to find out who was available and at what cost. Also, to see if the materials were here in Manhattan or had to be ordered first. It took me two days to answer all these questions and to have a signed contract. Remarkably, not a single person of the large number of workmen required for this project hesitated. All said yes to showing up at the appointed time in the middle of the night to do their part. When the day came, everything went like clockwork. It was orchestrated like a stage production. Demolition, pick-up of trash from the sidewalk, delivery of materials, flooring, wood, specialty epoxy floor finish and commercial box fans to the sidewalk. Installation, sanding, setting up the box fans to move fresh air to the workers, applying alcohol-based epoxy floor finish designed to cure in two hours. It all happened exactly as planned and the project was finished at six o'clock sharp. The time was exactly nine hours, not a minute to spare or wasted. In my experience I can think of no other place in the world where one can find this level of commitment and quality of quiet collaboration.

Only In New York City, where the logo is:

"We keep trying until we get it right." The City grows on you. There was also fun in the City. Especially around Washington Square Park, the NYU campus and the lower east side where fashion spies take pictures of what folks are wearing to plan their collections for the upcoming season. People were dancing under the Arch with their big wheel roller skates with the big rubber wheels and the blocks that absorb the shock of big wheels on rough surfaces. I had to have a pair of those. Once I owned mine, I tried them out on one of the City's blistering hot July days, wearing nothing but sports trunks and a tank top plus of course my brand-new roller skates. It felt good to create some wind, while rolling on my test run down third Avenue towards Cooper Union. I was amazed how fast these wheels were and I made movements I would make while skiing on groomed hard packed snow. The sidewalk I was travelling on had some cracks in it and with my accelerating speed the sections between cracks seemed to be getting shorter and shorter until my little hop across one crack landed me right in front of another one. I had to lift off immediately. To my surprise, as I was lifted by my movement, rebound from my skate's big soft wheels took me way up into the air, made me fly much higher and farther than intended. It would have landed me inside the next intersection the view into which was obstructed by a big box van. Now I did something I knew from skiing. I put my left skate down and began to negotiate a sharp right-hand turn in mid-air. This works fine on skis. On skates not so much. I touched down with the rear wheels of my left skate now moving sideways. I landed on my side into the sound of a thud and a snap. When I looked, I saw my left foot pointing east while my leg and chest were pointing west. A four-letter word escaped my lips. The very first people walking my way took out their cell phone and called for an ambulance. She took off a cardigan to support my neck and head and stayed with me until I was safely in the rescue vehicle and on my way to the hospital.

New Yorkers rising to the occasion. The surgeon was very talented and two weeks and ten thousand dollars later with five breaks set and protected by a full-length cast I was standing at work running the checkout line at our store.

I was in extreme pain so I started to smoke because inhalation of smoke bothered me more than the pain. As a bonus I discovered that nicotine helped me to isolate the pain in my leg, so I was able to heal while working without using pain medication.

I was still in therapy at the time about my other life issues and the new advice was, that when I needed a break, I could just take one. Not necessary to break my body.

"Take care of yourself as others need to do the same for themselves. No more crossover assumption of responsibility." My therapist said. That was a new concept for me. I am sorry but memories come rushing in at times. We had contracted to renovate a "brownstone" west of Broadway. It is a four-story structure with a red sandstone stoop, wrought iron handrails and a lower level entry leading to what was once servant's quarters with access to a rectangular back yard. Doors and windows were framed with sculpted sandstone. The front walls were deep double walls allowing space for window seats with ornate wooden fold away shutters that disappeared into the paneling when opened. Our client came from Venezuela. He had purchased the property for his family to live here while his grand-children were getting their education. He came personally to lay out the upper floors. We snapped chalk lines suggesting walls and he approved the layout. We framed the walls. The next day he came and wanted the layout changed, now that he could see it in three dimensions. The following morning, he asked us to change the entire layout of the two upper floors for a second time. I told him that we would be happy to do all the changes for him, but that the contract was no longer a fixed price. It would have to be change ordered to become a time and materials contract. I also told him that I would have to bring new carpenters to do the work this time. He signed the change order. When we left the building after this site visit, I told the owner to step back so I could activate the burglar alarm.

"Why do you have an alarm?" he asked. "There is nothing in the building".

Yes sir, there is. On the roof. The HVAC unit is mounted to a pair of steel beams on the roof. We do not want it stolen." I explained. "Early this morning, burglars came and broke into every car on this block to remove electronic devices. When we came here all the alarms were sounding. Everyone seems to wait until the burglars are gone, before shutting off their alarms and calling the police. Even the police are being robbed. The other day a crew with official looking blue overalls, company suits with name tags. They walked into the New York City Police headquarters building, removed most of the copper roof, loaded it on their truck and left. No one suspected foul play until the next rain and no one could explain what happened to the roofing contractor. There had been no contract." Listening to these reports, the owner from Venezuela said:

"I am going to sell the building. We already live in a banana republic. I was intending to send my children and grand-children to a safer place. This, we have at home." He concluded the engagement with a termination settlement on his change order contract. The building was sold. We finished the renovations for new owners who Love New York just the way it is.

I walked home from a project along central park one day which took me close to the Dakota where John Lennon lived. Many people were assembled in the area and lit candles. Luminaries were appearing everywhere. A total stranger hugged me and through his tears told me that John Lennon had been shot. Grief was welling up all over the City. In the park more and more people were gathering holding one another. Even in grief, New York was standing together.

There was a transition time when I had new business in New York and ongoing business still on the Island. Every two Weeks I had to commute from La Guardia Airport. I discovered that my boarding pass was stamped in red 'destination unknown.' A small group of regulars met at a Midtown Manhattan Hotel for drinks, then took the Hotel Shuttle to LaGuardia Airport. A few drinks were helping us to relax while we placed bets on the outcome of today's flight and the 'unknown destination du jour.' Fog and weather on the Island was often causing delays or forcing planes to be diverted elsewhere. One day, fog on the Island and the Cape shut down air travel. Planes were cancelled. Standing next to me was a gentleman who was beside himself. He had left his newly-wed wife on the Island when his company called for his immediate return to attend a meeting in the City. He had not known how to tell them to call after his honeymoon. He had to get back to the Island now to see if he was still married. I too had to go. It was the Year of gasoline shortages.

"I have a car with a full tank of gas on 9th street in Manhattan," I told him. "You are welcome to join me if that helps you. We should be able to get you there by breakfast time tomorrow morning." We took off and made it all the way to Providence, Rhodes Island, where we ran out of gas. We were just able to pull into a gas station that did not say 'out of gas'. It even had the odd numbers today and my number plate had the required odd number. This gas station was still closed for another three hours. We were waiting at the pump. It was three o'clock in the morning. We were wired from fatigue. The station was going to open at six. We could get some shut eye. A police cruiser pulled up and stopped in front of us.

"License and registration," the officer demanded. I handed both to him. He returned the documents. "This gas station is closed," he said.

"I know," I replied.

"You are not supposed to be here," the officer said.

"We had no choice, Sir," I replied. "We are out of gas." He went back to his cruiser. When he returned, he said:

"Ok. You can stay here, but don't go anywhere." We were looking at each other, then at the gas gauge.

"Wanna go somewhere?" I asked, the minute the trooper was out of earshot. We burst out laughing so hard, tears were streaming down our faces. We finally got our fill of gasoline and were on our way to the harbor to catch our ferry. We were so tired that only our laughing fits kept us awake. "You will be on the first boat in any case," I told my companion. "You are going somewhere." One last burst of laughter. I lost him at the ticket counter. He boarded with his passenger ticket. I went into the standby line. I said a little prayer for their marriage. I never saw him again.

This time the commuter plane went to the Cape instead of directly to the Island. Then it flew to another Island. Here we deplaned. We were to connect with a flight out of Boston. When this plane finally landed, the arriving passengers were green in their faces. While waiting in the passenger lounge, the few of us had been discussing options to get to our Island. Maybe by boat? We learned that Water Street was under water and no one was willing to experience the very rough seas, or to swim to the boat. We decided to go by plane. If the plane goes, we go. We were used to this. We were stoic island-hopping commuters. We finally boarded and the small twin-engine Cessna took off for the Island. It was. operated by a single pilot. I was seated behind the pilot in a window seat. I had a good view at the instruments. I liked to observe the pilot's activities, the tuning of the engines and the setting of the trim. We ascended to just above four thousand feet, the cruising altitude from which we would almost immediately begin our descend for landing. Twenty minutes flight time at the most. The plane was being tossed around as we had expected. A few minutes into our flight I could see the pilot changing course. Suddenly the engines began to whine to a very high pitch. There seemed to be no air for the propellers to slice through. Strapped into my seat, I suddenly felt the bottom fall away. To my astonishment, the plane was staying in level position. I had my eyes on the instruments. The little plane was now plummeting so fast that everything that was not secured rose up as if in weightless space, to get stuck to the ceiling. I could feel the pull on my seatbelt. Instinctively I reached for the ceiling, to brace myself. My eyes were observing the altimeter. We were falling towards the ocean at a speed faster than free fall. The altimeter needle went around and around. I looked out of the window. I could see white caps on the ocean. They were approaching fast. We were going straight down, still level. I braced harder against the ceiling. Only seconds to impact. I was completely calm. I saw people holding hands. I asked myself:

"How do you feel now?" I answered: "Life was a spectacular ride. My entire life. Never a dull moment. Never a pause. Never less than the most amazing people to meet, places to be, things to do, obstacles to run up against, challenges to master." I asked myself: "How do you feel right now?" The answer was: "I feel grateful. I am in a deep state of peace and I have a feeling of luck: This fabulous ride will end very appropriately with a gigantic splash." I was almost giddy. Suddenly the engines slowed, propellers were getting purchase on air, catching resistance and the plane began to lurch forward. I suddenly felt heavy as lead in the seat of my chair. We were gaining forward motion, getting lifted. The waves were retreating. Loose objects were falling from the ceiling, as the altimeter was indicating gain in altitude. One course correction and we were approaching the runway. A normal unspectacular landing into the wind followed. We taxied off the runway and the plane came to a final stop. Everyone was breathing deeply, lost in thoughts, motionless, silence was ringing in my ears after the engines were turned off and the propellers had stopped. We had made it home. After what felt like a very long time, someone opened the passenger door from the outside and pulled down the stairs. I was stunned and a little unsure if I was really here. Passengers began leaving the plane and tentatively stepped onto the tarmac of the airport. I was the last one to deplane watching the pilot sitting still, his arms over his steering harness with his head resting on his forearms. He had not turned around, had not said the usual "thank you for flying Island Air and please fly with us again soon." He looked spent. I walked towards the airport building, approaching the fence behind which the luggage table is located. Before entering the enclosure, I stopped and turned around one more time, wondering what the pilot would do next. I saw no one boarding. For a long while there was no movement. Then an attendant went to close the passenger door after folding up the stairs. Still no movement in the plane. Still the pilot's arms over the controls his head down. I was waiting to see what he would do. Would he park the plane and never Fly again or would he go up there and have it out with the storm?

After what seemed to be an eternity, I noticed movement in the cockpit. The pilot was slowly sitting up. I watched him put on his head set and reach for overhead switches. He moved the microphone to his mouth. The engines turned over one by one and after a few moments the plane began to taxi towards the runway for takeoff. I stood still until the plane was airborne. It became quiet. Just the noise of the wind in the distance where we had come from.

I had said my goodbyes to the world not half an hour ago. I had been at peace with my fate, filled only with gratitude. I liked the idea of the big splash. I had decided it would have been a perfect ending of an amazing journey, the last ride of my life. Suddenly I realized: Here I was. Now what?"

Together with my trauma counsellor, I was now confronting the crashes from my past as they present themselves and at the same time I was dealing with a constant stream of new discoveries. We addressed them as they Presented themselves and as they arrived in my memory. A recurring item is my relationship with my father. I eventually went to see him. I wanted to know if he had any memory of domestic violence. I wanted to find a way to forgive him. I realized that untreated PTSD and his Projective Identity Disorder had made him blind to see who I am. He had been projecting his own image so strongly, that all he could see was how different I had turned out and how I was not a match. I had to say goodbye to him and to the idea that one day he might meet me and get to know me.

"I was more tolerant with him after letting him die in my mind. When he actually died, I had the experience of losing him all over again. Only this time his surviving children and our mother were together for ten days talking on and off around the clock. To my surprise I found that we were one family in name only. Each one of us had a different view about life in this family and feelings were as unique as we were. Ten survivors, ten stories. What was my discovery? I had been looking for my father all these years. I was still looking for him now. I realized something else: I had grown to believe that I could always find my way home no matter where I started out from or where I was going. There was one thing I had lost and was yet to find: Myself."

I was beginning to sense that the place I had to look was not the same as where I had been looking. I had to look inside my own heart, where I was all alone. And now that hurt.

CHAPTER TWENTY

BACK ON ISLAND

"My time in Manhattan was winding down. I was missing the Island, where even rain on hardtop seemed to be clean, where you could step close to the water and see the horizon, see ever changing colors, textures and movements. In Manhattan I had developed the horrible feeling of time being relentless and unstoppable. I felt the need to slow things down and to live life on my own terms and at my own pace. Looking back at this time now, I can see how lack of knowledge about myself was the result of years spent in pursuit of other people's agenda, of trying to realize other people's dreams. On my first day back on the island I ran into a friend who was wondering if I could raise a crew to do a renovation of an original Victorian building. He was the architect and part owner of the project. The challenge was to retain the charm of this old handcrafted farmhouse while giving it modern systems and appointments. I agreed to do it. It was rewarding both in terms of the outcome and because I was able to work with renaissance craftsmen who were able to replicate paneled wall systems and a fireplace surround in the living room with the same hand tools used two hundred years ago.

I had a conversation with the crew one day over coffee on the subject of dreams. The men spoke of trips, vehicles, education, homes and families. We had shared many ideas.

"How about I pay you on Mondays instead of Fridays," I proposed. "That way, instead of blowing your paycheck at the bar, you have all week to think about your dreams and come Friday, you spend only what is left." They liked the idea, and by the end of the project, most of the dreams were either realized or well on the way to becoming reality.

I found a new set of plans on my desk, that one of my friends was bidding on. When we had first met, we were both at the very bottom of the construction hierarchy. It was due to the generosity of this friend that I learned the construction language. I was inspired by his meticulous approach to each task. He would become one of the premier home builders of his generation. Now, he asked me to do a quantities take-off for materials and to give him a proposal for managing this project. We won the bid and soon went to work on one of the most beautiful houses I have ever built. This house was so well designed, that only two telephone conferences and one architect's visit were required to resolve final questions and to get approval on our work. I built an elevated footpath leading to a pond, creating a sweet spot on the water. During the final owner's inspection, the built-in sound system was being tested when I heard the third Mozart Horn Concerto in live volume played by Dennis Brain coming from the living room.

"Fabulous," I told the owner. "The acoustics work just as I thought."

"I want to give this set of CDs to you. A small thank you," the owner said.

The end of this project left me feeling sad and proud at once. I liked the fact that I did not have to live in all the houses I have built. Most of my projects were located on or near the shore. Designed by brilliant architects, who took advantage of the views while maintaining a low profile in the landscape. My skills were challenged and enhanced by the need for creative problem solving. I developed a habit of meditating about problems and matching solutions between three and five o'clock in the morning. One example was the completed flared granite stairwell to the driveway with a landing covered by a flat roof, supported by a pair of slender, exposed concrete columns. That day, these columns were to be poured into forms made of glued-up cardboard tubes. I visualized storm and rain pummeling my columns with fresh, wet concrete inside. They began swinging and bending and finally exploded pouring the concrete all over my light gray granite steps. On the way to the site I picked up bundles of pine strapping and rope to install reinforcements on the outside of the tubes. I covered the columns with tarps after the concrete was delivered and poured. Then it began to blow up a gale with bursts of heavy rain.

My favorite project on the Island was the gut renovation of a building on the harbor overlooking the harbor entrance and a lighthouse. Taking this turn of the century building apart, I could read the way it was built, finished and appointed. I found the original telephone wiring system, that connected neighborhood cottages, years before the rest of the Island had telephone service. What made this project special was that the owners were very engaged in the building process.

Another project was special to me because of the talent required to realize its unique design. It is a privilege to work side by side with talented woodworkers, masons and designers. The challenges of working on an island forced me to rise to seemingly insurmountable challenges requiring very special collaboration to meet them. First, we had to conduct an archeological dig to be sure no ancient burial ground was located at the site. They found artifacts from a fishing and hunting camp dating back 7500 years. When work began, the old camp became my construction office and a sheet of plywood became my desk and plan table. The plans called for a series of structures. A screened porch with a flat flared beamed ceiling and a floor paved in bluestone, followed by a foursquare great room with open floor plan at the center of which rises a round teepee style roof, topped by a clear story, followed by an integrated long house, placed on top of a one-story wall clad with light gray granite pavers with gable ends facing pond and upper grounds, covered by a bow roof. The plans asked for red cedar trim, tongue and groove cladding on living room walls and the teepee ceiling which is to be supported by a circle of white cedar columns, exposed rafters and four tall central columns at the center, supporting a fenestrated clear story above. The teepee roof and the perimeter trim are to be clad with gray lead coated copper, looking like fish scales. The central fireplace is to be set on a bluestone base matching the pavers of the exterior terrace. Four granite piers are to support matching gray lintels, forming a four-sided square mantle. The fireplace is to be visible from all four sides through glass doors. A central throat is to collect the smoke and lead it up though a stainless-steel chimney. From the granite mantle, a stacked trestle style tower of opposing red cedar four by four blocks is designed to reach the clear story as it narrows in width. This is to add a lacy wooden surround to soften the bright stainless chimney. The living room floor is to be finished with sanded oiled end grain blocks of tightly fitted four by four cedar pavers. The great room is to serve four purposes. An entry area, a kitchen, the dining set and a sitting area. Stepping up to a hallway opposite the screen porch is a centered stair tower which will divide the long house with a master suite at the water side to the west and bedrooms to the east. The stairs are to be built around a panel made of fir dowels beginning from the basement level to the top floor, woven with cedar strips forming a lacy central stair wall reminiscent of woven twig structures. The master bedroom is to have a built-in platform bed with a flared dreamcatcher canopy, radiating out from the headboard connected by woven branches. French doors are to lead to a water view deck. Railings are to be mounted to steel posts woven with opposing horizontal cedar strips. All elements reminiscent of Wampanoag native architecture, remnants of which were found in this region going back seven thousand five hundred years when the glaciers began melting back from here.

This award winning project was an education for me and its realization required a team of craftsmen with a great variety of outstanding skills. It was challenging to all participants. The home stretch will explain how much so. Leading up to completion were several tight spots:

The first came, when we learned that the honing machine for the Vermont mottled green slate counters was broken and replacement parts from Europe had to cleared through customs. Delivery of the counters was therefore pushed to a date unknown. In the excitement about finally finishing the counters, the manufacturer forgot to get a reservation for the ferry. The counters arrived at the port. I had to drive a pickup truck onto the ferry, waiting in standby. We made the transfer of the slate at a lumber yard on the mainland. I got back on the last ferry. We had crews standing by to meet the truck at the site, off load the slate counters and to begin installation immediately that night. It was now after eleven pm. The next morning plumbers, gas fitters, electricians and carpenters were lined up to install sinks, cooktop, outlets and cabinet doors. At nine o'clock am plumbers discovered that the two undermount sinks did not fit the manufactured holes in the counter. All hands were now tied until a fitting pair of sinks could be located. We searched the island and up and down the eastern seaboard. Finally, a pair of sinks was located in a warehouse in Connecticut. From there a driver was sent to deliver them to a small airport. We sent a private plane to bring the precious cargo to the Island. The sinks arrived at 4:30 in the afternoon. They were immediately installed, water, gas and electric connected, pots and pans placed in the cabinets and doors snapped into their hinges: The kitchen was now complete.

A few weeks earlier the architects had rejected three thousand square feet of bluestone pavers with natural cleft, because discolorations of iron oxide were visible and had not been culled out. A new batch of pavers had to be ordered. They arrived in port on the eve of the Fourth of July, the busiest day for the ferry in the entire year. The driver wanted to know how he was going to get on the ferry. He had no reservation. I had no answer for him, other than to stay put for the night. Spaces on the ferry are sold out months in advance of this date.

I went to bed with a deep sense of dread in the pit of my stomach and woke up at three am with a dry mouth. In my semi-state of wakefulness, I began thinking about companies that put trucks on steamship ferries. One after another I had to dismiss because none of the freight companies would have reservations they did not intend to use. Then it occurred to me. There was one exception: The grocery store. They just might. With my heart beating in my throat, I dialed the number of this store

149

at seven in the morning. I was preparing myself for a burst of laughter at the other end of the line. I began my plea:

"I know, this is probably the craziest thing you have ever heard. But by any chance you wouldn't have a reservation for a semi-trailer on the ferry this morning that you don't need?"

I could hardly breathe.

"Let me check" the voice said. After what seemed to be an eternity, the voice came back.

"As a matter of fact, I do. The number is XXXXXX under Name XXX. The nine o'clock ferry. It is for a large semi-trailer." With great relief, I exclaimed:

"You have just saved my day. No, you have saved my project. I don't know how to thank you".

"Pleasure", the voice said simply. Islanders helping islanders. All of us in the same boat.

The truck delivered the stone and the cutting and laying out of pavers could begin. The desired pattern began to emerge. The waterside terrace was last. The very last stone was laid one hour before the owners were scheduled to arrive. Stone dust was now being swept into the cracks between the pavers of the terrace.

The owners drove up to the house forty-five minutes early. After greeting them, I said:

"Why don't you take a walk down to the water. When you come back up, we will be ready for you." The owners agreed and walked down the hill to the waterfront of their land to look out over the pond.

Last minutes:

Landscapers were hydro-seeding the lawn, presenting green color out of which grass will soon sprout.

Masons sweeping stone dust into cracks on the terrace.

Decorators unpacking teak garden furniture for decks, terraces and the dining set for the screened porch.

Housekeepers loading bathroom cabinets, making up beds and vacuuming behind themselves on the way out, as they finish each room.

From the top down and from the inside out, packing materials are tumbling helter-skelter ahead of everyone and everything is being tossed into the back of a large box van.

The load contains leftover materials, tools, saws, protective covers, cardboard boxes and tissue paper.

The last thing to be tossed into the van are the vacuum cleaners.

The overhead door of the van is pulled shut.

Masons, plumbers, electricians, landscapers, decorators, carpenters and housekeepers leave ahead of the van.

I see the owners walking up to the house. I turn around.

All I can see are the two tail-lights of the van disappearing down the drive in a cloud of dust.

It is perfectly quiet. I hand the keys to the owners. "Welcome home."

Once in my truck, I stop at the end of the driveway to let the dust settle.

Suddenly a sense of grief is washing over me like a breaker on South Beach after a storm. Eighteen months of giving this project my all have come to an end.

Tomorrow I will have to remind my truck not to come here again.

My last project on Island was the replacement of a 'shingled cottage' at the waterfront near the harbor. The existing building had to be removed and a new one put up to serve the new owners for a long time to come. The new house was a shingled cottage similar to others near the harbor. It was equipped with state-of-the-art entertainment systems, a central electronics board, able to govern all functions from temperature of air and water to movie channels and sound equipment for audio and video to every room. Fiber optics were used for fast and secure communications and super-fast internet. This was the most sophisticated house we had ever built. It looked just like the original shingled cottages typical for this neighborhood.

When the time came for trim, interior and exterior moldings were ordered, made from Cyprus, a material used in many of the old houses in this neighborhood. Virtually rot proof.

The transformation that took place in the very end phase of this project was just short of magical. Landscape design was laid out and soil was raked, hardscape, walks and drives defined, stairs set and hedges planted. The lawn was rolled out over raked loam, placed like a carpet, giving an instant impression of a well-established estate. Simultaneously the trim was being painted white with the final coat and the house was ready for the final punch-list.

I insisted that kitchens and bathrooms had to be one hundred percent complete and in perfect working order. During my inspection of this kitchen I discovered that the gas cook-top was not igniting. It had to be replaced or repaired before the owner's arrival. The appliance vendor told me that he was unable to replace the cook-top until the following week, because he had no ferry reservation. I told him to look at his computer to see all the things we had bought from him over the years.

"Can you see the column on the right-hand side?" I asked him.

"Yes," he said.

"Now imagine there to be nothing but zeros. That is what you will see in the future if you cannot have a working cooktop here by ten o'clock on Saturday, installed and tested. It is up to you how you do this."

At nine o'clock Saturday morning I saw a speed boat run up on the sand bar at the beach in front of our project. A man climbed out, lifted a package and a small tool box out of the boat and walked up to the house. Fifteen minutes later the kitchen had a functioning cooktop. The boat was leaving a wake running out of the harbor and five hours later the owners found a fully functioning kitchen. Sure enough, the first thing she did was to turn on the gas flame of the cooktop.

She was amused when she saw the signs I had posted on all exterior doors. 'No Shoes.' A few weeks later, she told me that she had sent invitations for her housewarming party to her friends: "Come celebrate our new home with us. No Shoes."

Now in Maine by the side of the road, what was then a normal moment of joy, relief and pride turned in my mind's eye into endings. They felt like painful experiences as if I had been thrown out of my own house time and again. Now I had no response other than that this madness had to end. Again, and again I was all alone after having given to others all that I was able to give. I felt drained, exhausted and profoundly sad. I went on my way trying to make it through this day once my tears had stopped blinding me. I remember the good things also. The summer of 1991 our daughter was born. It was the year of Hurricane Bob. Topped that fall by the 'No Name Hurricane' that became also known as the Perfect Storm. Her arrival had given new meaning to everything I was doing. Living in a waterfront home made it imperative that our child was able to swim, was familiar with salt water, waves, currents and suddenly changing weather. Before she could walk, our baby learned how to float and right herself in the bathtub.

I had one desire for my child:

To keep her safe, to give her a good life.

Now she was my passenger in a head on collision with an impact speed of 120mph, that could have killed both of us. How could I forgive myself? Who cares that it was not my fault? How could I live with that?

I spent a summer with our two-year old girl. We went to the ocean every day, rain or shine. This was a wonderful experience. I will always be grateful for this time. Back on the Island we were lucky to enroll our child at a small private School, where she learned many life skills, interacted with other children and studied the basics of reading, writing and numbers. She had a large vocabulary and comprehension of words for her age. She was a curious child with peripheral orientation, aware of everything that was going on around her. She took events very much to heart. When she witnessed a terrible car accident during a commercial for the news, she felt empathy and the scene was not leaving her mind until the next day at kindergarten when she told her teacher that she had witnessed an accident. When the teacher called us to tell us that our daughter was lying about having seen an accident, we became aware of how intensely she was experiencing things and how much empathy she has. When she had reached the end of her private school time, we enrolled her in third grade at the primary school of our town. She had several friends at school who were born the same Year and whose parents had gotten to know us at prenatal parenting classes.

One day we were called in by her classroom teacher for a parent teacher conference. The teacher began speaking to our daughter's mother before I arrived. When I arrived, her mother was beside herself, in tears. This caught me by surprise and I wanted to know what was going on. I did not expect a teacher to have such an effect on a mother, unless there was something seriously wrong with a child. The teacher said:

"Your daughter has a learning disability"

"And you know that how?" I asked.

"She is looking around the classroom. We take that as a sign of attention deficit disorder. She cannot concentrate."

"What are you teaching right now?" I asked.

"The three Rs," she replied. "Reading, riting, rithmatic." She replied.

"And you are qualified to diagnose a learning disability in our child, how?" I inquired.

"There is a process," she replied. "We have a special needs track for children like your daughter. The State gives us funding for this program. $2400 dollars per child."

"You are teaching reading and writing and arithmetic?" I asked. "Did you know that our daughter had transferred from a private school and that she has already learned to read and write?"

"No, I was not aware of that." The teacher replied.

"Do I understand correctly then, that you have not seen our daughter's transcripts? Have you ever talked to her?" I followed up.

"Actually no, I have not seen her transcripts and I did not know where she had transferred from. We thought she had come from another Island." the teacher admitted.

"Have you ever spoken to her?"

"Actually, no." I was beginning to get sick to my stomach.

"What do you do for children with learning disabilities?" I asked.

"We give them Ritalin," she answered." The State pays for every child we put on the special needs track. We are a blue-ribbon school."

"And you are telling us that our child belongs on this track?"

"Yes." The teacher replied.

"Let me see," I repeated, "You had no idea our daughter came from a private school. You had no idea that she had already learned most of the material you are presently teaching. You never looked at her paperwork and you never spoke with her or took the time to get to know her." I was getting excited. "Before you called us in to tell us that our daughter has a learning disability for which you want to dispense drugs, our child learned to walk, swim, ride a bicycle, speak and understand English better than I can speak. In two years at her school, she has never given any of her teachers a reason for concern about her ability to learn. She is known to be helpful, polite, compassionate, circumspect and well spoken." I was getting more excited. "Now comes her third grade teacher, who has no idea who our child is and tells us that she wants to give her Ritalin, a known gateway drug to addiction for an illness, that was invented by a doctor in Great Britain, working for the makers of Ritalin in Europe, without producing any evidence that "learning disability" is a real disease that is treatable with drugs. He has confessed to this on his deathbed. He called it a hoax. And you fell for it, because such facts escape your attention." I was on fire now. "You have not presented our child for evaluation to someone qualified to make a determination of special needs. You are clearly over your head both legally and professionally when it comes to prescribing drugs to children. You have no license to diagnose or treat neurological or physical illnesses. You cannot even legally treat children for the common cold. You have missed every step in the order of events, after we have enrolled our child in your school. You suspect we are from another Island. We have paid property taxes in this town for almost twenty years. Everyone in this town, except you, knows who we are.

This is not what we have been paying into our school system for." I took another deep breath.

"If you had ever spoken to her, you would have found out that she has a very good command of the English language. She is able to explain the meaning of most words used in the New York Times to you. I would not be surprised if her active vocabulary is as large as yours. You are giving us your opinion about our child. You are suggesting that she can be helped with a State sponsored special needs program that will end her every chance in this society to get into secondary education and on top of this you propose to administer a known gateway drug for addiction without having any of the required qualifications to do so. No consultation with a physician, a psychiatrist, a neurologist or a learning specialist. Just drugs. That is all you have to suggest? This is a scandal. No. Do not interrupt me until I am finished. Before you throw our child under the bus, I have this to tell you. Our child does not have a learning disability. She may learn different from other children as all children do. I think when she was looking around, she was looking to see if any of her friends in your classroom needed her help. This is what she was taught to do at her previous school. She does not get bored. From what you have just told us, there is no evidence that our child has a learning disability. You have demonstrated that you have a teaching disability." I caught my breath.

"Now know this: We will never let our child set foot in your classroom again. We will find a school. She will be fine. Come after us and we will take this story public. Good day, ma'am." We immediately began looking for an alternative to this school. We had to leave this island.

We were hoping to find a community that is committed to educating children, rather than drugging them."

CHAPTER TWENTY ONE

MAINE

After the collision in Maine, when I found myself sinking into PTSD my child was eighteen years old. I was having trouble staying awake during the commencement ceremonies. I had undiagnosed sleep apnea which interrupted my sleep every two and a half minutes, preventing rest and REM sleep, causing my fast-declining health, loss of mobility and constantly rising levels of pain. I was unable to explain any of this to anyone. I felt tolerated at best. Being tolerated feels like an insult to someone who once had a life. I wanted to put an end to my new and useless existence. In my failing state, completion did not mean success, just another ending. I have to tell you both parts of my story. The one that shows how I functioned and the one that shows how I failed.

"We put our house on the market and began the search for a new community to live, work and educate our daughter. We scouted as far west as Lake Tahoe and deep into Maine where we discovered a small community where you could put 120 paper luminaries on the curb of main street, light the candles for Christmas and find them all still in perfect condition the next morning. I had never seen a community with such a low level of anger in the children. The town had a beautiful library, one of the oldest YMCAs with indoor swimming facilities in the country and in their parks department they maintained a ski resort with a chair lift and rope tow for the children and the community. It requires two hundred volunteers to stay open six days a week during the Winter. I became one of the volunteers with the National Ski Patrol. We had found our future home town. Soon thereafter a house was found.

"It is just like the house on the Island, facing East to the Sunrise, but on a beautiful pond," my ladies reported. "No jelly fish in the water."

"Buy it", I said after listening to the descriptions. "Make a full price offer and have a purchase and sale agreement signed before Friday. I will make it into what we need it to be." The owners accepted our offer and took the house off the market. The house was located at the west side of a 500-acre pond, had a grassy beach and a dock. The property came with a screened in gazebo on top of a rock the size of a house and a bunk house that used to be a tiny school house in the days of General Knox. To one side there was a trail through a stand of Aspens, reminiscent of a tiny piece of Appalachian trail. Vegetated also with tall firs, cedars, birches, fiddlehead ferns, orchids, mushrooms and mosses, the botanical diversity of coastal mountain vegetation was surrounding the house like a fuzzy green blanket. The previous owners had created boardwalks and gardens all around the house, offering views of flowerbeds, trumpet vine, roses and rhododendrons from every window. Lawns surrounding the grounds were bound by rock steps leading to the forest. I told my daughter and her mother that I expected there to be a long line of cars of interested, potential bidders by Friday. Fortunately, we had a purchase and sales agreement in place on Thursday and the owner simply sent everyone away after posting a "sold "sign at the top of the drive.

This was a first step to prepare our move to Maine. The sellers were not able to vacate the property as planned. They rented it back from us while we were living temporarily near Augusta Maine. Once again, I had a chance to spend time with our daughter, while her mother worked in a state office as its new director.

Our child and I went to the coast to explore the beach area of Penobscot Bay near our new home. We went to see a summer camp run by the University of Maine by a river in our watershed into which our lake drains. Here she would be able to attend summer camp. First as a participant and later as a camp counsellor. Together we were now learning about our watershed. Our pond was one of the tributaries of a protected salmon stream. We enrolled our daughter at a small private school in mid coast Maine, which was dedicated to preserving and promoting children's natural love for learning and discovery.

Once the property became available, massive rehab work had to be done. Replacing floors, cladding walls with pine, enlarging windows and finishing the upstairs of the garage to add guest quarters and an office space. Before leaving the Island, I had suffered a work accident. I now had to repair a double hernia after we arrived in Maine. I also had developed a condition in which my body was no longer able to absorb vitamin B12 from my diet. No food could be digested and a state of starvation had set in which was threatening my body with terminal collapse of vital systems. I was told by my doctor that this was a long-term stress condition. He ordered me to change my work to a less stressful engagement, perhaps a change in location. Fortunately, this was what we were doing. I learned to self-inject B12 and had the hernias repaired soon after the move to Maine.

Being laid up was forcing me to have to hire help to work on our house. The company I chose was the one that returned my calls, met with me promptly and produced good proposals for the work. I was especially impressed, when the lead carpenter told me that he had worked for this group for more than twenty years. Also impressive was the fact, that such a highly qualified mechanic was doing handyman work. A wise choice by management.

During one of the site meetings, the project supervisor told me she believed she was building an office for the competition.

"Yes you are, ma'm," I told her. At the end of the week during a punch list meeting I said:

"If you hire me, I don't have to compete with you". Two weeks later I received a call:

"Would you be interested to come in to meet the managers, the vice president and the president of the company, so we can show you what our company is doing? We would like to give you a tour of ongoing work, during which we have a chance to talk with you about joining our company." The good impression this company had made on me was now confirmed. I was more interested in working with them than going into competition with them.

It is a company chartered to do residential, commercial and steel construction. Their new venture was their home repair service, which had just completed the work at my house and done it very well. The company was set up as a profit-sharing company that even paid their employees sick leave and vacations. No surprise, that they had loyal employees and a very low turnover rate. Managers were holding weekly scheduled meetings, to discuss issues from project questions to technical challenges to inter-departmental collaboration and training opportunities. The culture of job safety was being coordinated with insurance companies and safety training was done regularly. I was impressed. To the question of what I thought about the home repair service, I answered that while repair service was the highest risk sector in the construction field, it could be the best advertising for a company, as it had been the case with my own project.

They offered me the job of leading this service. I accepted, even though this division was grossing only a fraction of what would be needed to pay my salary or to show a profit. This did not worry me at this point. What I saw was a solid talent pool and good potential. If done properly, we could serve every house in this town and far beyond. It was not a question "if" we would work on a house, but "when". It took us one year to do ten times the business from the one before and another two years when the company handed me a congratulatory plaque for reaching a million dollars in sales.

This did not happen like a nice little family of best friends. I was the new kid on the block and other managers were not always pleased and considered me competition, until bonuses were awarded and our home repair service success was being shared with them. I requested to be given white Vans with the company logo and the words Home Repair Service" printed in large letters on its sides. These vans were to be equipped and stocked with personal tools, company owned power- and pneumatic equipment and basic supplies, to cut down on trips to supply houses. This gave us the face of a professional service. Paired with a culture of mutual respect and support. During a team meeting, I told my new associates:

"We work as a team in people's homes. If I hear a leading carpenter scold or belittle another mechanic for asking a question or for asking for help, I will have to let him go, no matter what kind of rock star he is. There is no such thing as a stupid question. There is zero tolerance for insulting a co-worker or a customer. I want this workplace to be a safe zone for all of us and for our clients. See yourselves as promise keepers working for our clients."

This worked well for everyone and the crew were seen consulting with one another rather than barking out orders, forcing obedience or pulling rank. They called for help when they were out of their comfort zone. We thanked them and soon someone would show up, who was good at this task and quietly disappear after the challenge had been met and the detail was done correctly. I expanded the work of my team by hiring specialty subcontractors to do roofing, electrical work, plumbing, tile work, sidewall and other specialty projects. When I requested an assistant to answer the phone and to help me with paperwork such as developing proposals and work orders, other managers laughed out loud, exclaiming that they too wanted a secretary. I gave them a choice between my meeting customers in the field, helping our mechanics by solving problems, or sitting in the office doing what I did not do best. Paperwork. We chose the former. We were now making a living. I wanted the language of proposals, work orders and invoices to be identical. My assistant helped me to achieve this. She also was the voice that greeted potential customers. We changed the purpose of the home repair team to be that of promise keepers. Together we were doing repairs on people's homes, solved problems and gave advice.

I was not to be considered to be anyone's boss but to be everyone's helper, making sure that each and every promise we made was kept. The customer was boss. Most of our customers were women and disrespect for women was reason for immediate dismissal.

We were advancing skills and provided training to our team. To this end, we moved individuals to work on residential building projects, where they had a chance to practice and develop skills like hanging and adjusting windows and doors, insulating and flashing in tricky situations and solving condensation and vapor problems. In case of disagreements, our mechanics were asked to walk away from customers out of ear shot and to talk. Failing to find a resolution, they were encouraged to call me and I would facilitate a meeting over coffee.

Committed to be problem solvers, we were refusing to hide problems or to cover them up. We worked relentlessly at completing our task lists, leaving premises cleaner than we found them. We often inherited disappointment from customers bad experiences with other renovators. Punch list items were therefore done immediately. Extra work requests were answered with a call to the office to check if there was time to add the task and what it would cost to do so. As a result, our team showed up to work a few minutes early to finish their coffee and chat. When work started, we were on our client's time clock and we took this very seriously. Correspondingly, I protected our people from being insulted by customers. We declined to do work that neither our crews nor the company could stand behind like hiding problems cosmetically with trim or siding for "house flippers." Our customers asked frequently how come there was no foreman on our jobs and why it was, that the mechanics were consulting with each other rather than following orders.

"The work-order they have is verbatim the same as the proposal we submitted to you." I answered. "The order in which the work is performed is usually the same, unless the team can see a better way. Together they decide who does what. Decisions are made as a team. They are working for you. We aim for 100% completion in the shortest possible time with the least possible disturbance to your life. Once in a while you may see other mechanics show up to help or you see me step in to boost the team so we can keep our promises." I explained.

During my career as a builder, I have continuously read books on construction and taken at least one four-day seminar on leadership, motivation or team building each Year. In home repair we encounter hidden problems or discover genius ideas installed by craftsmen who came before us. We are challenged by elements such as frost, vapor, water, mold and decay. We sometimes have to correct design errors. This requires building trust with our customers.

We had to be cautious not to engage with our clients in matters of taste, style, or even to get overly friendly. We tried to keep our presence in our client's homes professional, to keep from turning our visits into social calls. No subjects other than task related issues were encouraged to be discussed during work hours. Politics and religion were considered personal themes to be talked about on personal time, preferably after work. We did not tolerate any form of discrimination.

My influence at managers meetings was informed by training in Mediation which I have received by participating in studies on negotiation and from volunteering in community mediation. I never managed to change the meeting style to be 'facilitated' meetings, which in my mind could have benefitted the company by flushing out all ideas and utilizing all the talent assembled around the table. I did succeed in ending the managers habit of conducting more than one conversation at a time. I also made a point of asking people who were always quiet about their thoughts. I made sure, that someone who had been interrupted, was asked to finish what they were trying to say. All this did not prevent me from having to work on overcoming resistance from other managers. Every morning, I did a meditation between five and six o'clock. I made a mental list of the people I would have interactions with this day. There were two possibilities with each interaction: Either they were going to be supportive and helpful. I would thank them in my mind; or they were going to oppose me and disagree with me. I also thanked them in my mind for forcing me to be a better communicator, for having to make better arguments, for having to be better prepared and for having to work harder to prove them wrong. My experience of working with some of the most demanding clients, architects and builders helped me.

Outside of work, there were a number of activities in Maine that caught my attention and gave me opportunities to volunteer: Our daughter's education was at the heart of my involvement in the community. To raise funds, I worked the concession stand during swim team home meets, serving food to participants and their families after partnering with local grocery stores and businesses for donations of ingredients and financial support for our sports teams. Sports were giving our children and their parents opportunities to meet and make friends with people from all parts of Maine and from all walks of life.

A small ski resort in the region fascinated me. A community ski resort that requires a couple of hundred trained volunteers to provide children and community with a safe center for winter sport activities six days a week. They trained and qualified me as a member of the ski patrol, a first responders training, including the skill to set and stabilize fractured bones, transport patients on a toboggan and to evacuate skiers from ski lifts during a power failure or other emergency. Even the use of CPR and defibrillators was taught. I enjoyed this association with "salt of the earth" people as much as I appreciated it.

I joined a lake association, a group of people concerned with the health of our pristine ponds which are part of our local watershed. These associations support training for invasive plant and -fish monitors, do water sampling and take water clarity measurements. Some associations maintain dams in good working order, complete with a fish ladders that support the alewife migration into the pond. I participated in a salmon recovery and protection effort in collaboration with biologists from the University of Maine. A land trust had purchased property along salmon streams and negotiated with property owners to place parcels next to salmon rivers under protective easements, governing best practices for the salmon river environment and land management. I was able to report observations about wildlife from Bald Eagles, Ospreys, Mountain Lions and Moose to Loons- to the editor and writer of a nature publication.

I was engaged as a River Keeper in our watershed. This educational effort was designed to bring fishermen and anglers on board, to help understanding, protecting and increase the salmon population, which was slowly beginning to make a come-back in response to these efforts. One major project was an attempt to slow the spread of Japanese knotweed, which can out-grow and smother all native plant species. Trash collection was another volunteer activity, as was the seasonal reporting of any changes in the river bed and surrounding area to biologists at the University of Maine. Very rewarding was the collaboration with first and second grade students in setting up tanks with salmon row for the children to observe the hatching of eggs and the ultimate timely return of the tiny fish to the proper streams, where these eggs had been laid and fertilized. Through these activities, children now "owned" their rivers and their fish.

I was proud to be asked to serve on Lakes and Ponds Committees, which was a community service reporting observations and raising development issues to the community, making policy suggestions to properly reconcile interests of a healthy environment, while supporting the building department, persuading property owners from building highly fertilized, perfect lawns with too much use of toxic pesticides between their homes and our pristine waters, which had attracted them to our community in the first place."

Now I was broken hearted at the loss of this
perfect world. I could not see it any more.
One day I was functioning at the fullest of my capabilities
and suddenly I was dropped onto a steep slope with nothing
holding my slide to a place I had not known before and was not
able to understand or control. Was my life just a fantasy, was
there a parallel reality, that was hidden from me? I searched for
opportunities to see better, to understand better. Why did I not
see this coming? Why was I completely unprepared? What would
be the benefit of going through all this again and visiting all of
this? Did I even have a choice? What did I have to do to stop it?

CHAPTER TWENTY-TWO

WHY?

"As an aspiring musician, French horn in hand I had visited fourteen countries. Art galleries were my favorite hang-out, because I never had money. Art exhibits were elegant, interesting and presented in beautiful buildings. Sometimes I was paid a lot of money. Then I spent a lot of money. I knew how to find the best and most expensive things to buy. I liked to share the bounty with friends. I lived large and travelled far. Hungry for magic moments that can stay with me forever. Now the tables were turned: Now came pain. Now came suffering.

Having to leave a Country in the dark of night and succeeding was a success then. Now it came back at me as heartbreak. I am sure I left broken hearts in my wake. Africa was hauntingly beautiful, the people who were suppressed were mesmerizing me with music and dance I witnessed and my shock of another departure was now coming home. Why was I feeling these things now? Why did my past come back to me scrambled and mixed up? What made it seem unstoppable? Why can I not talk to the ones who love me? Why do I sense this irritation at my being unable to just stop this nonsense and be normal again? Why am I getting physically worse all the time? Why do I feel so profoundly tired?

In Africa, the person who thought of killing a bushman as something to do for sport was a very good musician and as an eighteen-year old student I had seen him as a mentor and a friend. Not as a murderer. There was betrayal in this. Betrayal of Principle. Betrayal of Mankind. Betrayal of Truth. As I investigated further, I found, that Apartheid was not just a mandate to keep the white people from intermarrying with non-whites or Africans, who lived there by permission, serving their masters at their pleasure, wearing white, freshly pressed uniforms around people's homes, looking stunningly beautiful, but it was racism, a belief of superiority, that made everyone with pigmented skin into the product of a previous step of evolution. White pigmentation of skin was seen as something superior. Science has since exposed this as nonsense. We are all humans. Nauseatingly, only people with low self-esteem and the worst education can still espouse this view. Unfortunately, they also agree to the right to bear arms. And not surprisingly, they proclaim to be the keepers of the moral high ground on top of the hill. Here came my outrage over this humanitarian misconduct and yet another betrayal of my value system, as I take all racial discrimination as a personal insult. I was unable to breathe then and found myself unable to breathe now.

I soon came to realize that playing music was not giving me answers to the questions I was asking. I felt that there was something more important to do with my life. Now the filter of my shocked mind let the heartbreak come through. My awareness of a humanitarian crisis with unresolved social issues rose to a level that I could no longer tolerate.

Former chemical war factories were now transforming war poisons into agriculture products, convincing ignorant public officials to proclaim that it was a precondition to feeding mankind that these poisons were sprayed on food crops. No word that their own research had shown that these poisons did endanger the biodiversity of nature, compromise food security for humans and posed a detriment to public health.

The consequence of this knowledge was the development of genetically engineered seeds and organisms that were immune to their poisons. Now they are telling us that genetically modified organisms are safe. It is all a hoax. They want to control all the seed. Governments are complicit. Next, they will have to modify humans to be immune to their poisons. Roundup ready sperm owned by Monsanto and Bayer?

Another hoax was the so called 'cold war' waged with the help of fear mongers for the benefit of investors in the weapons industry. We were told lies by oil-, gas- and coal industrialists who were competing for dominance with nuclear power generating plants. Instead of serving the public, they were threatening the public while endangering the environment and the security of civilians everywhere. Grabbing as big a piece of the economic pie as they could by influencing public spending was the name of the game. Now the planet was beginning to burn up.

PTSD put me into a tailspin of conflict. If I were to survive, I had to go after the answer to the question: Where do I belong? Why is it that I cannot believe what everyone else seems to believe? Why am I insulted by nuclear power stations that pose a threat no smaller than nuclear weapons to mankind? Why am

I not trusting the motivation behind the 'financing of the Nazi
regime' or the 'financing of the economic post war boom?'

Why was I upset about the imprisonment of the East German
population behind a wall, while the industrial boom in the West of
Germany was being fueled with natural gas from Siberia? Why is it
all verifying itself when we sell war proposals with fake evidence and
intelligent people seem to concur? Why do we let the professionally
engineered 'world trade center take-down' kill thousands of innocent
citizens and hold no one to account for treason and domestic terror?
Why do we look on quietly, as the Patriot Act is being presented
as an answer to this event? Impaling civil liberties for security?

Why do we listen quietly when we are told that personal freedom
has to be curtailed if we were to be safe? At the same time,
why are we making millions of people homeless by financing
questionable wars? Why are we listening to people who ask for
trillions in military spending while proclaiming that we have
no money to raise our children or to feed and educate them?

Why do we vote for people who think they have jurisdiction
over retirement needs of our elders, or over the Social
Security Trust-Fund? Why is all of this making me so
profoundly upset now? Have we all gone insane?"

CHAPTER TWENTY-THREE

DROWNING

"Back in Bavaria my great aunt had told me in detail how a brave new world was being designed and nurtured, how such ideas had inspired a small group of young people who had been sent by their parents to a large farm for a summer vacation. The purpose of this Youth camp was to create an opportunity for Catholic and Protestant teenagers to meet, get acquainted and to become friends. The parents of these children were concerned about the polarization of people of different faiths. Populations who were moving across borders to seek better economic opportunities for themselves, following promises that were made to them by their leaders.

All this had suddenly come to light in the wake of explosive industrialization. The movement of great masses of people towards jobs in industry with very primitive housing and almost no social services existent at the time, both in Europe and in the 'free' world was generating anxiety in local people as well as in immigrant communities.

These parents believed that this unnatural divide could lead to civil war (as it was the case in Ireland for seventy-five years.) They felt unprepared to control the sudden shift of power from 'nobility ownership of the world', to industrial ownership of resources and humans. There was confusion. People still believed that colonies were places with natural and human resources, free for the taking and racism was aligned with purposeful exploitation. Local native populations who were willing to work for colonial invaders had a future; those opposing invaders were doomed, driven off their land or simply killed. The world was at a hair trigger point where all of this had to be sorted out. Two world wars followed, sending all the hopes and dreams of these young people into the incinerator of violence and hate.

I learned that these young people were dreaming of a world without racism or religious strife. This is where a plan was hatched to try building a 'new world order'. Not a new religion, but a new social order that nurtured humans from the beginning of their lives to their natural end as individuals with a full package of rights. They were looking to build a world for stakeholders instead of shareholders. They did not trust the justification of injustice with a higher standard of living for a few.

They wanted to offer education instead of oppression, participation instead of segregation. Grant humanitarian rights instead of sexual, national or tribal separation. They wanted to build social and economic justice for all without any of the labels still under discussion. We had Long conversations about farming in Africa which reminded me of a book I had read in the early sixties. Rachel Carson's "Silent Spring" had made me curious about whether or not it was possible to feed mankind without poisoning the planet in the process.

Before my music Season was over, my aunt had introduced me to a gentleman, who was the head of an agriculture school in Holland. He told me that Nature was an excellent teacher and that he would go to Canada and work in a meat packing plant to earn money, then he would purchase land and be a farmer trained by Canada's own soil. Can food be produced to feed mankind without committing collective suicide in the process? The answer was still out but agriculture was led to believe that the answer was no.

Here was another betrayal that I was now unable to process or to forget. It was haunting me. I went to study agriculture. With the help of friends, we began holding seminars for university students and farm workers on farms to explain the reality of producing real food, including preparing and serving meals. At the time this effort was very well received."

Now I was seeing everything through the filter of PTSD. I was devastated by the fact that all this seemed to have been a total failure. As my pain kept rising, I was confronted by insurmountable mental obstacles. I discovered a lack of flight response in myself. And my fight was just about gone as well. This all was bigger than me. I was not part of the solution, so I began seeing myself as part of the problem. I was not needed here anymore. Losing my life seemed to be a good conclusion. Nothing had ever felt as painful as everything did right now by the side of the road splashing around my life in fast forward, crying uncontrollably.

"Back on the Island I had stood many times at the ocean's edge where I had been washed ashore. I wanted to go home. Now it felt like I had another chance. I should have walked right into the water then and faded away. Now this thought was sweet, tempting and strangely acceptable. Back then I set out on my American Journey which now had landed me by the side of the road crying uncontrollably. Something began to happen in my mind. I suddenly had the idea that I was the problem of my failed life and that I had to find a way to redeem myself and to make it all better for those I loved. My mind began drifting as I drove from job appointments to the office and to my home.

I knew now that my ability to support my family or to do my job was slipping away. I noticed that I was causing irritation at home and that I was growing allergic to suggestions made to me that started with:

"You should just" or "you only have to" or "why can't you simply" or "why don't you just." I did not have any answers to the question 'Why'.

Fearing the loss of my job and my family, I developed an anxiety that landed me in the hospital with 220 pulses per minute. In full consciousness I watched the hospital emergency system call for code blue. I saw people rushing around when I was not responding to the medications the doctors had injected and now, they decided to stop my heart. They had to make me unconscious so they could defibrillate me and then send me by Ambulance to Maine's cardiology. I felt that I was no longer met with empathy. The exception was my daughter, who was able to understand my condition better than anyone else and who could just be there for me. She, of course, had been in the car with me when we crashed, a fact that was at the time a much bigger problem for me than my physical condition. Right or wrong, I felt I was no longer treated with love, care or patience. I began to feel the irritation I was causing and I began to sense that I was seen as selfish, self-absorbed, wallowing in narcissistic self-pity and self-imposed isolation, guilty of shutting everyone out, being unavailable, no longer participating in family life. Yes, I was sitting in front of the TV after work, not able to move even the remote control. I was completely spent. I was all alone. I had lost everything. I was unable to say to myself or to the members of my family that each day was a harder struggle than the day before and that I was completely exhausted. I was also immersed in trying to pull it all back together.

To make the problem complete I was losing my memory. I believed I was sleeping no more than one hour at a time while in reality my sleep was interrupted every two and a half minutes. I had not reached rem sleep for a long time. I was profoundly and deeply tired. I refused to take pain or sleep medications. I did not use any other type of self-medication. I was now living in a symphony of revolving pain, spasms and muscle cramps that would at times "checkmate" me. It felt like different areas of my body were holding off from revealing the severity of my injuries until one center of pain was healed enough to let the next one come to call. Chest (ribcage), left shoulder (torn rotator cuff), wrist (severe bone bruising), knees (cartilage damage and soft tissue damage), both shins (bone bruises), ankles, hips, back, neck all bruised. In other words, I was discovering a seemingly endless sequence of things that needed repair while for fourteen months the Workman's Compensation Insurance refused to accept that the accident as a work injury. I was struggling with health insurance, deductibles and unbelievable co-pays. I was facing losing the house. I would have defaulted on mortgage payments, were it not for the generosity of my family who sent me rescue checks. Meanwhile I kept on struggling. Early each morning I got up before everyone else, made coffee, took the trash out and drove off to work.

But now unconsciously, while driving down the road, I began looking at trees, curves in the road, telephone poles, rocks, ditches, embankments and bodies of water. My mind began calculating all the things my life insurance could pay for. I found out later, that my wife, who was the keeper of the money, had lapsed payments on this insurance and it had expired. I caught myself thinking these thoughts. I was not happy that my mind was going off on this terminal train of thought which I would not take for long on my own. I was a stoic person. Optimistic rather than depressive.

"This is crazy" I told myself:" You are going crazy" I warned myself. "I am tired. I am not strong enough. I want this fight to end. It is too hard" I told myself. "You need help now" I concluded for myself. As soon as I had a free hour, I walked into my physician's office without an appointment. I sat there until he was free to see me and started by saying:

"I am having these thoughts, and I don't like them". I walked into my house with a prescription in my hand, which he had called in to the pharmacist. That night I read the label and the descriptions of possible side effects and warnings. I found that just like in the TV adds, one of the side effects was suicide. Another betrayal.

"Why was everyone so happy to see me gone?" I got mad. I was back at the doctor's office as soon as he was open the following day:

"You surely must be joking," I told the doctor. "You gave me a drug to prevent me from killing myself, that has a suicide warning on the fact sheet. I am not using this drug. I need a therapist who can help me without drugs." I said in a very irritated tone. After I had calmed down, I handed him the pills and the doctor referred me to a therapist. I knew him as a client of my construction services. He knew me well. He knew how I functioned before the crash.

Finally, I was in good care. He was well regarded as a counselor, he was also part of the Wounded Warriors Project, where he provided counselling for traumatized veterans returning from foreign wars and for their families.

CHAPTER TWENTY-FOUR

THERAPY

I began seeing the counsellor twice a week after hearing his evaluation of my condition:

"You have a classic case of Post-Traumatic Stress Disorder", he said. "I am a Vietnam Veteran, injured and traumatized; I was treated and have learned to live a productive life." He stated. "Now it is my work to help trauma victims," he continued. "Your case is in a number of ways related to this. You are the son and grandson of traumatized veterans from WW1 and WW2. You have big T's, small T's and "inherited benefits" from your father, your mother and your grandparents". He said. "You grew up, surrounded by people with PTSD and those with "inherited benefits". None of them had any idea what was going on with them. Most have memory loss, some develop a sophisticated system of denial, almost a coping mechanism, some are also diagnosed for bi-polar disorder and many have combinations of these conditions." He continued: "You are from Europe. So was my family. Everyone from our parent and grandparent generation in Europe, with very few exceptions, was traumatized by war.

No one was treated correctly. The science came ten years later. I had the good fortune to be diagnosed and received treatment and counselling for PTSD from the U.S Veterans Administration after I returned from Vietnam.

It had not been until after the Korean War, that PTSD was isolated, defined and treated. After Vietnam there was already more knowledge available on the subject. We were becoming more successful in helping patients develop coping skills. Veterans are slowly beginning to reach out for help. We still have a long way to go. The stigma of 'disorder' is a powerful deterrent to reaching out for help. In sports, outdoor activities and growing up in a macho-man culture, get up and shake it off and ignore the pain is still a widespread standard. There is another large blind spot: Family and community.

We are now including entire families in treatment. There is no way for the families of trauma victims to fathom what has happened to their loved ones. I do not believe in re-traumatizing patients. We will address each issue as it arises.

You have suffered big trauma several times in your life, starting at age three with a third-degree burn. You also have suffered a number of little trauma events, such as accidents, betrayals and minor conflicts, plus you have inherited benefits like many people who are raised by parents with untreated PTSD. All of these trauma events have now been reactivated. That is why you feel like the world is falling on your head. Your parents and grand-parents trauma was never diagnosed or treated. But there is hope for you." He concluded.

I told him that I was concerned about the future of my family.

"I had invited my wife to attend our sessions, but she said that we did not have marital or family Issues. Therefore, she declined. The fact that our child was in the accident did not count as a related issue, nor did it seem to matter to her how I felt. I think she was right. These were separate issues only linked by the coincidence of this accident."

"We will attempt to heal these trauma events as they reveal themselves. I like using a method called 'Emotional Freedom Technique' which is done with the use of tapping on certain meridian points of the body while addressing issues, beginning with a statement of self- love, self-acceptance and self-honor:

"I love, honor and accept myself just the way I am, even though-,now follows the statement of issues: Things we fear or make us concerned, worries, distress, injuries, pain, hurts of any kind, relationship issues, work related issues, losses, betrayals, anything at all. Everything can be addressed in this way. It can be done any time day or night and in response to stressful events. We will work on developing coping skills."

The therapist further explained:

"Words used can be for example: I love, honor and accept myself just the way I am, even though I have lost my life as I knew it in a head on collision. Or: I love, honor and accept myself just the way I am, even though I cannot forgive myself for driving my child into a life-threatening crash. I will do a number of these statements together with you, while you learn to locate the meridian points that we tap on with each item.

Meanwhile, by yourself, you can begin to write a list of all the items of concern to you. We tap on each meridian point eight times and take the item through all of these points, tapping as the words are spoken and the issue is named. You can re-write the list from time to time, to see what has happened. Sometimes smaller items disappear as we grow our coping skills. This is repeated until all meridian points have been tapped eight times each. It will soon be easy for you to do this at home or anywhere.

In clinical trials, this tapping method was found to lower pulse rates and to increase oxygen levels in the blood."

In this fashion we went to work, while the world kept on caving in around me. I moved the big items to the top of the list which began with over two hundred items and was getting longer as new problems, more pain and other concerns were emerging. Time was spent during my sessions to talk about new items emerging from daily events than from items flooding in on me from the past.

I felt fortunate to have this excellent coach, who would see me in person and also gave me consults over the phone as needed. I was lucky and blessed by my family and by friends who did not hesitate to hold me up when I was falling. I had music in my background that I could play from memory in my inner ear. I discovered that I had been surrounded by my community of the last forty Years and I found generous support at every turn, including personal training and workouts in the water. I was able to visit geo-thermal spas with joint experts directing aquatic exercises in the south of Germany.

Once my worker's compensation insurance conceded, that this accident was work related, (fourteen months after I filed the claim), I was able to seek more specific accident related medical help. I had not been getting better despite my daily efforts, but was sliding into ever new physical and mental problems. In August of 2009 my physician sent me back to the surgeon who had seen me after the accident in January of that Year. This time the head surgeon looked at my MRI. He told me that the rotator cuff in my left shoulder had been torn.

"You need an operation." He said. "This can be repaired, but not with rehab work." As I had suspected, they did not want to operate on my shoulder because the insurance was only covering rehab work with copays. The doctors had failed to discuss that with me. They were not interested in helping me. They were milking my personal health insurance. I was livid.

It was now eight Months after the accident. I had been sent by his team into rehab with their physical therapist at their own facility. I exercised my heart out in the pool every day, as I was instructed to do. Now I pledged to him, that I would never set foot in this office again. That I was going to find a real orthopedic surgeon.

It took until July of 2010 to find the right surgeon and to get an appointment for an operation in Maine, followed by nine months of rehab. Meanwhile, my health was in an imperceptible, but steady decline. The generosity of my co-workers to step in for me in my declining mobility, to make inspections and to explain building failures to me, was deeply appreciated.

CHAPTER TWENTY-FIVE

MOTHER

While I was awaiting shoulder surgery, I decided to travel to Germany to see my eighty-six-year-old mother who was living in an assisted living facility near Hamburg, Germany. She had been battling Alzheimer's dementia. Physically, she was amazingly fit, aided by her habit of stretching in the morning and after resting and taking long, fast walks every day. No one knew how far her walks took her.

During my visit I was hoping to have her show me where she went. She agreed to take me on her walk. During our walk, the wind picked up and the temperature dropped to sub- zero. I had to ask her to return us to her home before we would get frostbite. She refused to wear hats. She regularly removed hoods from her winter jackets. "Hoods and hats are silly". She said. She would hide them. Then throw them out. Mother had a great love for the surrounding landscape, its plantings, forests, wild flowers and gardens. She loved rocks and semi-precious stones, collected them and brought them home to her room. We learned a lot from talking to the many people she had met on her walks and interacted with. We also learned from people who had given her rides home at dinner time, when she was too far away to make it home in time. At her senior home she liked to play the guitar, whistle tunes or sing with other seniors. All she needed was a short prompt of a melody or lyrics.

Now we sat in her living room and had tea. I was still trying to find out how to reach her through the blockage that prevented information to enter her short-term memory.

Cozy in the warmth of her room, holding cups of tea, we found in front of us on the coffee table an old framed family photo.

"I am having a little difficulty with my memory lately," she said. "I left this picture on the table to remind me to ask you: Who are the people in this picture?"

I looked closely at the image. It was a picture of her family. It showed my grandparents with several of their children. There was no date. Judging by the age of the children present, it must have been taken during the mid- to late nineteen twenties. Mother was the third oldest of six children born to our grandparents. In this image, my grandmother is wearing a white, ankle length dress with a white, lace fringed apron. Her dark brown hair is put up in a large bun. My Grandfather is wearing a formal waistcoat, white shirt and tie, gray riding britches and black, polished riding boots. He has a stern look on his face. He served as a mounted cavalry officer during WWI. In this image the grownups are surrounded by their four beautiful girls, dressed in white with black little shoes, sitting and standing to form a perfect family circle. I said:

"This is your Family. Sometime in the late twenties. I think you are the one sitting in front left." She said:

"Oh, I must have forgotten. I have become really forgetful lately, you know."

"Would you like me to tell you about your family?" I asked.

"Yes", she replied, "that would be very nice of You". She addressed me with the formal You which told me, that at this moment she did not know who I was.

For the next two and a half hours I spoke about our family.

"This is your Family, sometime in the late twenties" I repeated. "I think you are the one sitting in front left." I told her everything I could remember, everything I was told, everything I have experienced myself. I simply told the story as it came to my mind. At some point I saw that she had her eyes closed. I asked:

"Am I putting you to sleep?"

"No", she replied, "I am imagining, what you are telling me. I have not been this awake in a very long time, please go on". When I was finished with my story, she got up and gave me a long, tight hug.

"I thank you," she said into my ear, holding me tightly. Mother was rather private with her emotions. Her Generation was tough like hardened steel, they had to be. It was a requirement for survivors of her time. The recollections of mother had been the primary source of what I knew about our origins. Her extended family was the canvas upon which the lives of her parents and siblings were painted. It had also shaped the tone and atmosphere in our home as we grew up with her, while our father was at war and detained as a POW, followed by another five-year separation until the housing shortage could be resolved. The heartbreak over the loss of loved ones, friends, neighbors, spouses and children, physical and emotional injuries and endless separations were buried deep under the rubble of all the emergencies of daily life.

My mothers life has spanned the time from the early nineteen twenties to the summer of two thousand and eleven. She died with Alzheimer's dementia after she went missing in a 400 square mile forest in June of 2011. She was found after fifty days in a location of her choosing where she had sat down at the edge of a field overlooking yellow blossoms. The 20-acre field was bounded by tall windrows of her beloved oak, willow, poplar and maple trees. She had remained untouched by people or animals for fifty days. She had simply sunk back into the garments she was wearing at the time of her departure from our life. The place where she had been seen last and where rescue dogs had followed her trail, was ten miles distant from where she was found. A massive search effort was started immediately by the missing persons department. I assisted the search with great diligence. I did not find her body. Her spirit was looking at me from every flower, every tree, every stone, every blade of grass and every animal I encountered. I felt privileged to be part of the search team. She returned to where she had come from, guided by the Angel who had brought her here. She was at peace. She longed to be reunited with those she loved. She knew to find them in the spirit world. For her memorial service in a meadow that was at the heart of the forest she loved, we read poems she had written and had given us permission to look at after she departed. Her wish was honored. She would finally be reunited with the love of her life. My parents had started their journey together in an unbelievably romantic love relationship. They exchanged daily letters and married immediately after her graduation from High School. During the war and some turbulent post war years, she proceeded to move time and again with her growing family, giving birth to a child about every other year for twenty years, while father finished service as a field surgeon during the war. He had found a position as co-founder, teacher and physician at a new school, taught at a Teachers Training Seminar, wrote a textbook for teachers and founded protective workshops and living facilities for disabled individuals. Both my parents were mission- driven. They had survived the Nazi Regime against many odds, (there is not a single word of reference to the Nazi Regime in their correspondence.) The Nazis had shut down grandfather's church, raided his library and burned his books in a public square. This young couple had no reason to believe that this dangerous movement would go away overnight without a fight. They pledged stand their ground.

The fight they were not able to win was everyone's untreated PTSD, which mother did not recognize, because she too grew up with a father suffering from PTSD with the same type of episodes.

PTSD ultimately broke my parents apart. The man she loved more than life went off to war and never returned. I grew up at a dinner table, where the question of freedom was discussed all the time. Our parents knew that the establishment of a string of nuclear power plants from one end of the country to the other was rendering the German Federal Republic militarily un-defendable. Still in shock from experiences during and after the second world war with human rights abuses inherent to armed conflict, our parents were very concerned about the loss of freedom by subordination of information systems, education, research and the economy to the interests of international corporations and governments with agendas other than the well-being of private citizens. Our parents were committed to fighting for Freedom. That is why they stayed in Country. Chancellor Adenauer had won his election on the platform of an unarmed, neutral Germany. Minister Erhard knew how to promote an "economic miracle" based upon a newly equipped industry with well- trained engineers, mechanics and workers. In private however, Adenauer was already negotiating for the first sixty thousand fully equipped troops for an army that could not defend its own country because of civil nuclear proliferation.

In their prayers my parents had been hoping to see Germany remain neutral and unarmed. This plan was not to be. They redoubled their commitment to education and the quest for freedom. Growing up under this avalanche of very serious concerns was a challenge for me, because I also had an identity to discover and a life to live. I could not simply be attached by default to all the problems of the world. I did not always feel like being well known. At times I felt that I was competing against a world that kept intruding with all its importance and urgent needs into my important world of being a child. Of course I did not know at the time that my parents had grown up in a world that was one gigantic emergency. Therefore they had no clue what to say to children in a normal world. They had no role-model for parenting. They had PTSD and inherited benefits from their traumatized parents and from their own experiences.

In my parents dreams children were expected to come to Earth as messengers from the Spirit World with new answers. By the time we finally did speak, it was clear that our parents did not remember that we were supposed to be the ones with the compass and the roadmap. Instead we were the ones who had to learn to be quiet when grownups were speaking and they spoke all the time. Growing up our parents had experienced our grand-parents, who were desperately trying to find out how to lead their parishioners and their children through this valley of evil, to keep them from losing faith in a world at war for two generations. As I listen to my siblings tell about moments when our father was actually paying attention to us personally, I realize that we are all talking about very rare occasions. Such moments became bigger than life in our memory. He was struggling with something big in his persona, that caused him to explode. These episodes had clearly nothing to do with us. They were episodes of untreated PTSD. As children in the care of our mother before our family could be united, we were living in the world of King Arthur. We knew all about Percival and the quest for the Holy Grail. Girls tore off a sleeve from their garments and pinned them to the shield of their young knight, who would go out and get it shredded and bloodied in valiant battle for the girl's honor, sending every loser home to the maiden to serve her until the young knight finally returned home. That night the girl would get to "feel" the wounds and lay herbs upon them before bathing the nights tired limbs and laying down with the valiant night in bloody armor, for warmth and comfort, to heal the hardships that came with riding on horseback in suits of metal armor, carrying long jousting poles with flags attached for identification and a shield with the girl's sleeve hanging torn and limp. These girls would give the night a child nine months later. (This was my sex education.)

When I lived in America Years later and a co- worker told me at coffee time on Monday that he had gotten laid that weekend, I knew what he meant.

Following my parents separation, Mother wrote and published her own ideas under a pseudonym still assuming that no one would want to hear from a house-wife with ten children. She made remarkable suggestions regarding the advance of social justice, liberty and freedom of self-determination as well as developing and expressing thoughts about communication in the development of sustainable social systems. Her thinking was practical and wise. It is an important work that will become beneficial as soon as her students begin engaging in- and continuing the discussions she has started while raising her ten children. It was tragic that her husband failed to support her in her writing efforts. He took her presence and support for granted. He finally even forgot to give her credit for the essential role she had played not only as the mother of his ten children but as a partner and collaborator in his educational, medical, social science and poetic writing efforts. Perhaps the fact that both were children of ministers informed the role of the wife as a servant to a greater purpose in the husband's life. This and untreated PTSD ultimately cost them their marriage.

PTSD and inherited benefits which remained undiagnosed and untreated until the late nineteen fifties did not get the needed recognition and treatment in my life until after my own injuries in 2008.

We have learned a number of important lessons from my mother:

"More important than giving fast answers is to formulate good questions. Herein lie the seeds out of which will grow good answers," she would say. She had an innate ability to take different points of view into consideration. She was able to show respect to people from cultures other than her own, religions and nationalities from around the globe. This ability would prompt her to develop methods of social inquest with inclusive and uniting elements. Her insistence upon the development of social justice was uncompromising. She demanded the discovery of principles of purpose for political appointees rather than the replacement of people by a democratic process without consensus about what needed to be accomplished. She would say:

"If a train is on the wrong track, running in the wrong direction, it does not make sense to vote on replacing the driver". She wanted to find answers based upon the merits of issues rather than on the principle divisions by party affiliation. She could not see a way into a future free of violent conflict, without consensus. And she rejected violence as an option for governance.

I will add a few lines of Mother's thoughts here in her memory: I paraphrase.

"These modern times, we are the inheritors of, are not very old: From the Year 1800 to 2000 new ideas have evolved. Many were tried for the first time. Boundaries were moved, broken or dismissed in every field of human endeavor. Old and tried systems in Society and Technology were abandoned or altered based upon new thinking, scientific discovery or infra-structure improvements that would alter people's lives and introduce new expectations. People living during the nineteenth Century set developments in motion that have taken the world from the village with horses and oxen to the age of manned travel to the moon. We are looking at the universe from the universe now. We are re-visiting microbiology and have a greater understanding of biodiversity. Many of these achievements were driven in the service of warfare. The struggle for power has become more brutal and deadly than ever before. The past one hundred and fifty years have seen more people dislocated, more homes and communities destroyed and rebuilt, more individuals of every age group and nationality traumatized, displaced and brutalized than ever before. More lives were lost by human hands. Yet the world population has exploded in numbers as food production was improved. The poorest and most desperate people seem to have seen the greatest population explosions. Today the world is still struggling with the concepts of liberty, freedom, social justice, and environmental justice, because with few exceptions there is no mandate in the charter of corporations to serve the public. They are chartered to make money for investors. Wars financed by the public are a false economy but the experience is that much progress was made during war efforts. We are conditioned to trust the idea that military progress and innovation is good for civilians and communities and that wars are necessary to guarantee the freedom of progress. Consumers have no idea that their choices are what pays for all decisions and products corporations make. Economic Growth and Competitiveness have become the mantra of the day, while sustainability, social responsibility and environmental protection are seen as a liability. So far we have no experience or reference to real peace time economy. We still follow the military model. That is why leading nations have overspent their budgets on proxy-wars. Consumer products are made primarily in countries that ignore the environmental impact of industrial activity, despite universal knowledge of the lethal consequences. Do the math. Continuous growth is a hoax. If you have just arrived here on planet Earth you will hear people argue about whether or not climate change was caused by human activity. A debate that makes one group of scientists look ridiculous and another feel bad. At the end of the day it makes little difference who is right and who is wrong, because water that used to turn to snow and form glaciers on top of mountains and on both poles is now melting and rivers that were fed from the steady supply of water from glaciers above, have started to stay dry. That will shut the most populated regions on Earth down for lack of water. First, they are flooding during rains because the watershed is dry and deforested and does not hold water. Storms raging from oceans have become more frequent and destructive. Ocean levels have begun to rise, corresponding to the melting of ice caps at both poles. Unsustainable management practices in the use of natural resources such as forests, soil, air and water, have disguised changes for a while and now scientists, who have not been silenced by politicians and governments representing industry, are in agreement that changes are in progress that will be difficult to reverse and impossible to manage in the future unless repairs start right now. We are in the middle of global climate change that is about to cause a series of humanitarian disasters that will require a reversal of attitudes from selfish, local, partisan argumentation to generous, international, inclusive participatory problem solving, based on a global perspective and accomplished through principled leadership.

One day I wish that we can all act on the knowledge, that all decisions matter everywhere on this planet. What might be helpful is that our young generation is using communication on the internet, with cell-phones with cameras, live streaming capability, computers and satellite services to connect the planet at an instant. That generation has begun to connect people around the world in real time. It is getting more difficult to make up stories about invented enemies, false flag attacks, or to hide deal-making of interest groups who benefit from water destruction, non-recoverable resource exploitation and -depletion. This is a generation that can rally worldwide in an instant. Ideas are spreading fast and influence peddling has become more difficult, because there is no longer only a local forum but an international one. Ideas of independence are common and the rewards of creative thought, constructive action and problem solving are the talk of the day. All this will help when the environment begins calling the inhabitants of this planet to task. This is the generation that realizes that it is not smart to buy things we do not need, with money we do not have, to impress people we do not like.

As these words are written, the world is struggling to cope with challenges in the global economy and financial markets. It appears as though global finance is the last resort to mine for power and control, without proven purpose to serve those who actually do things to create value. Social Security and Pension funds entrusted to governments are being raided and the cash-flow from taxes has been leveraged to a point that we have mortgaged our children's future. The income is migrating upwards to the top one percent of the population, who have become used to evade tax payments to the point where some are asking to pay more taxes because they can see no future in the way things are being handled. Emerging Nations who used to be part of the third world, are now embracing solar energy production, competing in the production of goods and services for world markets and are the new players in the international struggle for power and control. Everyone is exporting more goods than importing. They have ordered sophisticated weapons systems for security, which our own weapons industry gladly provides and exports in the name of security. These former third world nations, like China and Indonesia are giving considerable credit to former leading nations, which they have used to finance their military adventures. Insolvency is no longer only a problem for countries like Turkey, Greece, Portugal, Italy and Spain, but the USA, France, the U.K., Germany and Switzerland are challenged by deficits that they can never repay. The specter of the failure of regulatory decisions and international banking practices has become palatable. This is reminiscent of the time of the Stuarts in England before the British East India Company was chartered to go and raid the riches of the East for the benefit of Empire. The difference today is, that there is no place left to plunder. We have done it. It took about two centuries of greed and now we have to talk and listen to one another, to see if together we can reconstruct things in a sustainable way, that works for all of us, including the environment which is in acute crisis now.

I am an optimist. I think it can be done. Why is all this mentioned here, and what does it have to do with this story? To me, this is important, because what happened in the past and what will happen in the future is the result of our thinking and our sense of responsibility and integration. Advances in knowledge have changed the focus from insular thinking to global understanding and cosmic observation. Events that have taken place during the period we are looking at and the lessons that can be taken away are fascinating. We have learned to see the planet as one living organism. The human population as one of many species that occupy this planet in symbiosis with all other forms of life and the responsibility of our actions is to be mindful that everything we do will have an impact upon every other part of this organism.

We also know that this does not mean that all humans will have to speak one language and wear uniforms. It means that we can see that the diversity of languages, customs, art and individual expression of thought, philosophy, religion and music as part and parcel of the diversity that makes this planet work, similar to biodiversity in nature.

We cannot afford to compromise our biosphere by seeing ourselves isolated as part of something else. At the end of a hundred and fifty years of rapid evolution of ideas, technology, chemistry, biology and resulting possibilities, brought on by vastly improved understanding of ecosystems, people can now reevaluate the methodology of problem-solving and decision- making.

Despite the fact that a struggle is playing out between monopolistic powers wishing for scientists to disappear and knowledge to be hidden and not shared, we are blessed with smart people who continue to improve listening and communication skills. They are advancing what they believe and if we are lucky will give us a livable planet for the future.

We can trust the process of consensus building and consensus-based dispute resolution. We know that there is more power in information sharing than in the formation of monopolies and that there is more value in inclusion than in exploitation. We have good evidence about what works and what does not work. We have means to communicate and be in touch with each other in real time around the globe.

That is the world that can give us hope.

A world full of traumatized people is a word in need of healing. The truth is this: Violent Conflict Resolution has become a thing of the past. No problem has ever been solved using violence, because there is no resolution. There is only perpetuation. Violent conflict is expensive and can only be justified by those who are having a stake in the outcome. Weapons proliferation is never about peace. Weapons production is not value creation; therefore, it is not an economic activity. We know what the real cost of war is. It is costing us a livable planet. We know we cannot afford it. This is my answer to the messages I received from my mother, while she was raising ten children:

May we never abandon the quest for knowledge. Let us make use of what we have learned. Let us go back to work for the benefit of families, communities and nations for whom we are willing to lay down our lives. Let us find another way. A way without wars.

My mother has reminded us, that as living organisms, we share our origin with all other life. We must therefore start by granting each other the highest respect and to share the right to life with all other life in this universe.

It is important to appreciate the fact that each person has a unique view on the world. It is interesting to find out what that is. It will help us to redefine human rights which will likely be a work in progress for some time to come. No social justice can be achieved as long as human rights are violated.

Mother's prayer
mark with flowers the invisible trail
do it now, do it for all, wait and see who will hail
if it's a wanderer, give help, no delay
give food and some flowers to send on the way.
approaches the king in the height of his might,
leave the rose in the dust, do the honors him right.
Approaches your lover in hurrying gate,
give roses, give all him, yourself and your fate.
Come death, break your bread, give him thanks, say amen.
Let him lead with strong hand to the land whence we came,
Leave no roses behind, see in moments of bliss.
In their soft woven gowns, open wide to us all
a glimpse of eternity, designed not to fall.

Behold my dear heart, the chalice is full
it is endowed with the ultimate gift.
Keep it filled and let time and again
this gem of creation share all of its blessings,
let it always achieve the sacrament of loving souls,
the eternal, merciful powers in the grace of your guidance
through this darkness of life. Let the spark it still holds
light the fires of love, so the spirit can lead to the spirit we are.

CHAPTER TWENTY-SIX

GLOBAL PTSD

Wars are creating a problem that is not well understood. Too many of our young soldiers come home from combat only to end their own lives because they found themselves unable to reconnect with their former lives and fell into depression, isolation and failure. Many trauma victims are not able to learn coping- mechanisms in time to keep them from destroying their own lives and in doing so, the lives of the people they love and who love them. The number of post-combat casualties have rarely been accurately established, but estimates have exceeded the number of casualties in the war theater and combat related activities by a factor of ten. According to the department of defense, every single day more than twenty of our Veterans end their lives by their own weapons. It is shocking to note the difference in language, used in reference to our young people going into combat to "defend our freedom and our way of life" versus the language used to describe unemployable desperate Veterans who end up homeless in the streets of our cities or who live hidden someplace with their own families unemployable and disabled. We now try to make them responsible for causing pollution.

Many Veterans keep applying to be redeployed again and again because they believe that combat is a place where they belong. Here they know they can function. Here they have brothers and partners who understand them and here they are not alone. Some communities have now begun to outlaw giving assistance to homeless Veterans and outrageously, some cities have begun bulldozing tiny house colonies that have made life for a few more bearable by giving them a little more than temporary tarpaulins for shelter.

Most suffer from PTSD.

Post-Traumatic Stress Disorder is probably one of the most widespread health problems today. At the same time it is also one of the most treatable conditions, where the benefit of treatment is far greater than the cost. Not affordable is the price society pays in failed lives, including the harm done in "inherited benefits" to spouses, children and relatives of victims of PTSD. We are spreading the victimization by making society calloused by seeing the tragedy unfold right on the streets of our cities and by declaring bankruptcy in facing this challenge.

PTSD is common in veterans of war, as well as amongst first responders, fire service personnel, rescue and recovery specialists and police. During and after two world wars, countless people were forced to react to circumstances rather than being able to create their own lives. People are traumatized by loss of control, loss of home or country.

Once communities stood together using rules, customs, culture and discipline to gather strength and build the resiliency necessary to withstand the pyroclastic flow of events that threaten to incinerate them and wash them away.

Criminalizing individuals who self-medicate to ease the pain and end up falling into addiction was inadequate then and is inadequate now. It serves only the interests of private prison operators and corrupt judges.

To understand our parents, grandparents and great-grandparents and their reaction to events of the twentieth century and the present, we have to ask: What was the frame of reference that inspired their sense of duty and responsibility, what influenced the choices they made when forced to react? No time in History has forced more families to flee to save their lives, never before have more people taken to the road to migrate away from harm. The UN now estimates seventy million refugees in need of rescue. They are victims of war.

That number does not include climate refugees, driven from their homes by severe weather events.

We see fascists and the extreme right as well as religious extremists gaining political traction in search for control. The element in common is the feeling of being left behind and disenfranchised by existing governments. More violence as preached by them is not the answer.

Never before has re-settlement of people for economic-, political- or religious reasons, inflicted more harm, isolation or distrust. Destruction of property, theft and plundering have traumatized civilians in unprecedented numbers. Lives ended through combat whenever civilians are used as human shields, points to the absurdity of violent conflict and war.

It achieves a state of numbness and worn out empathy.

Someone is making these weapons; someone is making the bullets and someone is paying for them. Too many are paying with their lives for the profits of a few. Civilian targets were left out of war theaters until WWII. This changed with air-raids against cities and civilian targets. They were perpetrated by all sides of the conflict, multiplying loss of life and the incident of traumatization exponentially, causing an avalanche of victims of PTSD. Military leaders who ordered these air-raids against civilians, claimed that this was the only way to end war forever. What it did accomplish was to perpetuate the willingness of young people to be radicalized, given the availability of money and weapons. It certainly accomplished one other thing:

A wider distribution of PTSD and the inherent victimization of entire generations of non-combatants including women and children who suffer from what is now called "inherited benefits".

Today wars are started, planned and paid for with borrowed money, while we win elections with the slogan of no new taxes. (We see tax credits given to corporations who sponsor unqualified leaders for office, protecting their interests. We used to call this bribery and corruption). These budgets are being justified as protecting our interests, meaning the interests of resource-based industries such as energy and manufacturing. We don't just trade. We take what we need, then protect what we have. Anywhere in the world. We call anyone who disagrees with these actions a terrorist. We are still using license of empire building similar to Rome and the British Empire. Crimes against Humanity are being committed right in plain sight for all to see.

Mothers, who have lost a child will tell you that each and every casualty from violent conflict is a crime against humanity. A constant stream of PTSD-victims is returning home from combat, bringing trauma home to their unsuspecting spouses and children. One day we will have to forgive ourselves for permitting anyone to send young daughters and sons into combat. We will have to forgive ourselves for letting our tax money be misused for war, while the needs of our communities, our veterans, our elders and our children are being ignored and marginalized.

We pay twenty times more for war than for education We pay twice as much for incarceration than for college education and send our scholars into life with a debt as great as a mortgage was for a home for their parents. We must get serious about repairing the damage we have done to entire families now. As long as there is the false promise of an economic dividend in the pursuit of violent conflict, nonviolent alternatives will not be discussed or considered earnestly. We need to recognize that only the weapons industry and their shareholders benefit from war.

We have to begin adding up the real cost of violence to society and to humanity. We are beginning to worry about the cost and size of government. We are seeing the global debt rise beyond dangerous levels. All we come up with is the idea of the need for more wars. Wars have ways of increasing the reasons why they are being fought: War on drugs, war on crime, war on cancer. war on opioid abuse, war on terrorism, to name a few. All are feeding on themselves without contributing to solutions.

Families of PTSD victims are in large part footing the bill for that which causes PTSD while personally paying the ultimate cost: The loss of loved ones who were supposed to be able to come home and function as they did before they left.

My focus of this part of the narrative is directed towards the search for ways to understand and to heal the wounds of war, of trauma and inherited benefits of spouses and children of people who go into harm's way in the service to the public, be it as soldiers, first responders, firefighters, surgeons or therapists even. They all become traumatized in their line of duty and will sooner or later need help. I would like to see a reduction in suffering from PTSD. This is not something we can delegate. I want to show how support networks have been successful and can be built on a grassroots level, that can make a difference going forward.

It is my hope that with better understanding of this ailment, the devastation it can inflict will be contained and become manageable. As people realize that they themselves can take charge of the rebuilding of individuals as well as of communities, one can begin and must never stop. We can and must mobilize all the talent we have so amply available in our own families. Have you looked at your kids lately? They are the best. They love you just the way you are. We can all follow their lead. I wish to see the shame about PTSD disappear. I wish for the reduction in suicides and for the end of devastating isolation in the midst of friends and loved ones. I wish to declare peace on PTSD. Together we can win this." People say.

"Winning is not everything". I say: "It is the only thing."

CHAPTER TWENTY-SEVEN

COPING SKILLS

I am the son of a veteran with PTSD. I had a number of ways to trigger my Dad. I have received very severe punishment for that. Now I have to make myself afraid. Call it risk management. Physical pain is not something I fear. I can tell it is there, but it does not affect my mood. It is there, it may buckle my legs if it is severe. It might make me faint. Pain sometimes leads to cramping. Cramping must be managed. PTSD must be managed. Like with cramps, we need coping skills. First we look it straight in the face. I am not afraid of pain, high places, people, animals, boats, cars or death. No fear. How come you ask? I look them straight in the face.

What I am afraid of, is disappointing people. Often there is not much I can do to avoid it, because I do not know what the expectations are. I am afraid of expressing my needs or to insist to have them met. This is a contract problem. I do not make good contracts for myself. I do well meeting my own needs when I am by myself, but often fail when I am with others. I am afraid of not listening well enough. I am afraid of being locked inside a house. I am afraid of being locked inside myself. I am afraid of betrayal. I am afraid of having my heart broken. It may break right back and kill me.

Yet I venture out. I know the reward is worth the risk.

People say:

"Living is not for the faint of heart. We have to live every day. We only have to die once." That is certainly the truth. It is tricky. I have PTSD. I had a big trauma event when I was three years old. I had several big trauma events when I was eleven and twelve years old. Many other trauma events took place and made me experience the sensation of dying, even. I had another big trauma event when I was struck by an oncoming truck in my lane. It is healing now. They all are healing now. I am building coping skills. The first one is, I know when I need to remove myself from a situation when I am at risk of getting triggered and I know when I need help.

Then I ask for help.

In the Spring of 2015, I realized one day that the best thing that could have happened to me was this head-on collision. It made me collide with my own PTSD and forced me to confront it. It made me confront inherited PTSD from my ancestors.

No drugs. Just meditation. In the water. In the woods. At the beach. In bed. No drugs. Another look at childhood and family. People ask me:

"Who are you?" This is a question that comes up now and then and as long as I can remember. The answer is:

"I am a survivor of PTSD. No drugs." People talk. I hear them talk mostly about others and least about themselves. I now must learn to forgive myself. Then others. No drugs. My professional life, my career, my learning process, forgive the betrayals. No drugs. More language comprehension. I made an observation about reacting to insults. In Germany I was immune to insults delivered in local accents. It did not trigger a reaction. I never gave it a thought. This changed when I was insulted in German by a Swiss person in America. It instantly triggered a reaction in my brain. I had to learn to forgive. No drugs. First forgive myself, then the speaker of the insult.

Step one:

For you the first question will be:

Do you need to detox first? Alcohol, heroin, meth, crack, prescription drugs, other stuff you are addicted to?

Get help. Get on the wagon.

PTSD works against you as long as you self medicate.

Get help. Get your family into treatment with you. So they understand.

For me, PTSD kept coming up like waves. Again, and again. Shit. It is a Black Hole. The only way out is to go all the way down, through it and out the other side. Like undertow in a rip tide.

"Don't fight it", I tell myself. Relax. Breathe. Breathe. Breathe. Only I know what it means. There is no one I can say this to. They can't get it. They don't get me. Not anymore. They still talk to the man from yesterday. I can think or say anything, while my loved ones hear nothing. They think I don't care, they might say that it is not all about me. I have to face it. There is no one.

I am alone. No one understands. I am paranoid. I am no good to anybody anymore. I am struggling to get through the day without screwing up. I can't let my men down, I can't let my customers down, I can't let my company down, I can't let my wife down, I can't let my daughter down. I don't know how to forgive myself. Pull over. I can't see a thing. I am flooding.

All I can think of now is that I can't do this and I can't do that and I have no place to run and no place to hide. You don't get it that I would lay down my life for you, that I would kill for you, that I would go rogue, if someone hurts you.

Hello, where are you, can you hear me, hello, hello, anybody? Breathe… breathe… breathe. This will get better. Or will it? It must. I will make it better. I have done things. I can do stuff. I can, I will. Breathe. Breathe. Breathe. My mind is roaming. I cannot do this alone. I need help.

I went to get help. I am as strange a case as anyone has seen. We are all strange singular cases like our fingerprints, because there is only one road for each one of us. We all can find it, as long as we do not take drugs but ask for help.

I almost forgot. My dad beat me, whenever he caught me being "off his schedule" with the result that I can now endure more pain than anyone I know. During these episodes I stepped aside mentally and observed the proceedings unflinchingly, because to twitch would have caused further beatings. I returned to my own body when it was over. The reason I did not hate my dad for this abuse was, that I noticed that he also was beside himself during these events. Did anyone know?

My mother did. She chained me to the radiator like a dog with a thirty-foot chain. Chaining me to the building was mother's way of protecting me from being absent, when Dad came home. Back then, I was spared punishment at the loss of freedom. This is what they told us after 911 when they brought the Patriot Act.

What about now?
I am free to do whatever I want.
I am entitled to get help.
I am falling.
I hit bottom.
I begin to climb one little step at a time.
I am setting little achievable goals for myself.
I hear a dancer explain Tango.
Tango is a shared language.
It is trust, discipline, rhythm, attention.
Intuition, sensation, desire.
There are no lies.
There is just… the dance.
Steps are taken together.
No leader.
No follower.
One pays attention
and senses the partner's moves.
Tango is the lift I was reaching for.
Now I am.

201

CHAPTER TWENTY-EIGHT

GONE MISSING

It was three o'clock in the morning, when the phone rang.

"She went missing," the voice said. "I can't take it anymore. If one more person says 'did you look?' I will kill myself."

"Whow, whow, whow. Hold on. Tell me what happened. Start by 'who went missing'?" I replied.

"Our Mother." It stood in the air like a huge thunderhead.

"I tell you what," I said after what seemed an eternity. "Do nothing at all. I am on my way. I will take over, where you have left off. You have done more than anyone can be asked to do.

I will be there as soon as I can fly out. If you just hang in there until I get there. Please. We collected all the frequent flier's miles and put together a round trip for me with a return trip for mid-September.

Thirty hours later I arrived at his house. We talked for a long time. Before I went to sleep, I told him that for now I was doing the communicating with family and friends, giving updates and answering the phone. The next morning, we had an appointment with the director of the regional missing person's department. I was still under jet lag which made me appear very calm. The director began by reconfirming the garments our mother was wearing the day she was last seen. She proceeded to recount the day, the area, the interviews with witnesses. Then she handed us a map the canine search party had made following her scent. This map described a portion of a walk she had taken that day in a forest three times the size of Manhattan.

"We have the help from the police training academy. They made one hundred persons available to search the thickets of the forest shoulder to shoulder. We do not want to miss any clues. We also have alerted a riding stable. They have many riders on the trails in this area. Members of the missing persons department are riders in that stable. We have done several helicopter searches and are continuing. We found out that your mother was picked up by the Railroad police a couple months ago when she boarded a train trying to go see her mother in southern Germany. She had no ticket. She told police that she needed to go help her mother. The present search was immediately shared with railroad police, including her image. Also, the local papers have issued a missing person report. Most people we have interviewed know her."

We thanked her for her diligence and promised to let her know if we learned anything new. Once back at my brother's home, I contacted a friend at the Royal Mounted Police in Canada, who is a search and rescue expert. I asked him to stand by and coach me through my quest. He generously agreed. "24/7" He said. To have this coach was a critical support for me, no matter the outcome.

I went to get a new chip for my camera which I was planning to use with tele lens. Evenings I would spend enhancing my images taken with my tele lens to be sure I did not miss anything. I had the idea that somehow, I had to get into her head. I looked at her notes and in particular at a notebook with poems and prayers she had written some years back when she was in distress over the discovery, that even though her beloved husband had come home from the war, part of him never came back and was still missing.

She was in the process of throwing this notebook away. My brother intercepted it.

"You can have it." she said, "but I do not want you to look at it, until after I am gone."

"By all means, look at it now." My coach encouraged me. I was also looking at her medical record. She had recently been treated for a kidney insufficiency, which, according to my coach, could made her thirsty and cause extreme pain.

"Look for bodies of water. Any water." I bought a polarizing filter for my tele lens. I used a bicycle to ride to the search area about ten miles distant from our house. I began my search at her assisted living facility, trying to remember the walk our mother had pointed out to me when we last saw each other. Now it was mid-June and Gardens began to bloom. I decided to speak to her neighbors, knowing that she could never walk past a garden without congratulating the owners on their work. The first gardener was a woman in her fifties who was glad to meet another member of our mother's large family.

"You know, the first time I met your mother she was standing there holding up the head of a rose. When I asked her what she was doing, she said:

"I am giving this beautiful rose a rest. Maybe she will live another day."

"She continued to hold her rose while I went back to my work. I spoke often and at length with her. She is missed. Everyone likes her. I hope you will find her. This should not happen. Not to anyone."

I met many people along the trails that she took regularly all year. She was known for her very fast walking pace. The forester who told me that she was important to his life because she was the only person who ever paid him tribute for his work.

"You have the most beautiful forest," she had told him.

"That did not just make my day." He said. "Coming from this senior it made my career. I will never forget her. We are all very upset since she went missing. We are all looking for her. Good luck with your search." I spoke to the driver of a logging truck. He too was very upset. I was afraid he would hit me.

"This was not supposed to happen," he shouted over the sound of his big engine. "Not to her. She is one of us." I was speechless. He just drove off. As I spoke to many more people after introducing myself, I learned about the range of her walks. Ten miles, fifteen miles from her assisted living facility. No one at her home knew this. People in the forest had often given her rides back to her home, so she would not miss dinner.

They just dropped her off, so no one knew. Only once did it happen that she did not return. Her caregivers thought she was visiting family nearby. She was very secure in the outdoors and could easily make shelter for a night. No one ever found out, because with Alzheimer's, she had no recollection in her short-term memory. Talking to her most people had no idea she had Alzheimer's.

The Area in which she lived, was a large forest intensively managed with logging roads laid out in a grid, with quarters, that had topography like sand dunes with many interesting minerals, which she brought home in her pockets, now covering a one foot wide border around the building she was living in, since there was no place to put them all inside of her room.

The forest also had some wetlands and a canal which drains the adjacent farming area into the Elbe river some miles away. Some former gravel pits also contained water, some stocked with fish. Some of them private with high fences and gates. I went everywhere, looked at every body of water no matter how small. I was searching from the outside perimeter in, while search teams were still searching in concentric patterns from the center out. I saw the occasional helicopter flying slow passes. The farm fields I walked through were surrounded by hedge rows and some were surrounded by tall trees, interspersed by small tree nurseries and some orchards, lovely enough, that this entire area was a popular destination for evening walks and weekend picnics. The second week of my search I rented a tall SUV to make passes through the logging roads to be able to cover more ground in less time, using my camera's tele lens to increase my range. The pressure to find her was mounting by the day, even though my coach was telling me to hang in there.

"Do not count her out quite yet," he would say. Coming home empty-handed day after day left me in a state of deep exhaustion and depression. I had just had my knees operated on in the winter, a repair that was a result of a head on collision. I was still in treatment for PTSD. I was able to get counselling over the phone to keep me from falling apart in despair. Periodically I went to visit members of my mother's family to report and to connect and to see signs of family traditions that might give me fresh clues. One such journey was to see a cousin who was also the third child of a large family. My cousin had spent time at my grandfather's house. I was hoping we could have some long conversations about our family. To give us that time he invited me on a road trip through the Check Republic to Slovenia where he had business. In the proximity to Prague our vehicle was stolen with all our luggage, my computer, my notes of the search and some 8000 pictures I had on the camera and on flash drives. We reported the loss. The police helped us call a hotel and order some food to our room, since first they were taking us in for questioning with an interpreter. The interview lasted until three o'clock in the morning. When it was finally my turn, I stepped into the chief's office and asked him, why we were interrogated as if we had committed a crime. As I was about to sit down, I realized that the chair for the interviewee was rickety and very loose.

"This is not a chair". I told the interpreter.

"Yes, it is a chair" came the reply from the chief of detectives.

"Tell the chief", I said to the interpreter, "I am a safety officer and construction supervisor plus a first responder in the United States. If something happens to me at police head-quarters in the office of the chief of detectives, such as a chair collapsing, this will be no longer a case of a stolen car, but it will become an international incident of police negligence and abuse. If you wish to interview me, bring me a chair and I will answer your questions gladly. We can become friends instead." They brought me a normal, solid chair and I answered all his questions. When I left, we shook hands in friendship. Two days later the car was found in a four-square residential block, occupying two parking spaces behind a social club. The car was guarded by two officers, who were by now friendly with the little children who lived there. The passport of the driver was still in the car. Missing were only the computers and my camera equipment which had also been the focus of the interrogation. Earlier, on the way to the hotel, the young detective who drove us had told us that the police had trouble doing detective work because they were still working from the communist playbook, therefore the people distrusted them. I saw in my mind's eye the intimidation that came from sitting on a shaky chair during interrogation. I felt lucky to be at home in the USA.

As I visited mother's family members, I had asked permission to photograph their world. In return I off loaded all my pictures to their computers. From this source I was able to retrieve about two thousand images of my search for our mother.

On day twenty-five, my coach recommended to end rescue and to begin recovery. He prepared me for what I might find. I had this very strong feeling as I wandered around the search area that our mother was looking right back at me. That night when I came home to my brother, I said to him:

"We may not have found her body. I look at the stones she loved, the trees, the flowers, the grass, the deer, bunnies, birds, horses, everything in this amazing environment. I have the strong feeling that she is right there with me, looking back at me through everything she loved so much."

Finally, she was found by a farmer in his field as he was getting it ready for harvest, less than a mile from her home in a place that was away from foot traffic and could not be seen from the road. Here she had sat down facing east, where she could watch the stars come up over a twenty-acre field of yellow blossoms, surrounded by hundred-year- old trees. Here she awaited the Angel who had brought her to our world to come and guide her home. She would be united with her mother, her loved ones and the love of her life, our father.

The farmer gave us permission to create a small stone surround where she had rested, sunk back into her clothes for fifty days, miraculously untouched by animals including foxes, wolves, wild boar and birds of prey. At home we planted a tree in her honor of the variety she loved the most. Her ashes were interred at a meadow cemetery right where her favorite walk would lead us. In the circle of family and friends we recited some of her own poems and played music she loved.

Alzheimer's dementia had already taken part of her away from us. We remember her life as something truly amazing. We know now that we can reach her the same way we were able to reach her during Alzheimer's: Through her heart, using our hearts.

I now had a few days to await my flight home, a chance for me to visit with my next younger brother who was living near Freiburg in a winery of similar size as the winery our grand-parents family had owned. The day I arrived there I received an email announcing that my wife had filed for divorce.

This was more than I could handle. It took advantage of my PTSD and dropped me all the way down into a bottomless pit. I was sleepless for three days and three nights. I wrote these words:

Lost heart

Sing me the song of a heart that went missing
it left nothing but blindness and silence behind
like after a storm when the wind has stopped pressing
the thunder and lightning left deaf me and blind
how many times can my heart be broken
how many times will I think I will die
how many breaths have I left to be taken
before I can vanish with the sound of a sigh
when first I was walking a blond little boy
I went down to the river and returned full of joy
I had found the first mile of the trail that would lead
to the rest of the world that was my world in deed
how many ways can my poor heart be broken
how many times must I think I will die
how many heartbeats must I feel to be beating
before it will fade and in silence I lie
by the time I was ten we had moved fifteen times
leaving friends leaving places leaving rivers behind

what I took was the air was the rain was the light
was the darkness to hide from the eyes of the night
how many crashes can my heart still endure
how many heartbeats will it take for a cure
how many prayers can it say in a day
before it has said all it's able to say
it is fear of expression no words to explain
that can strangle the heart 'til no movements remain
now silence is all that is left to perceive
and no wizard can tell where and why did it leave
today the tsunami finally hit
it had been much too calm and the ocean had quit
now the trash in the current is shredding my life
into primary pieces no anger no strife
how many times can my heart still be broken
how many times will I think I will die
how many breaths will today I be taking
before I will drown and my tears will run dry
waking up on the shore of a land I don't know
I must learn like before to reopen the show
and embrace what is left of my dignity here
to reclaim what is mine and not crumble in fear
how many times can my poor heart be broken
how many versions of life can I try
how many mountains will I climb for the token
of hope that back down I can rest and not cry
I did try my hand at love with much passion
finding out what will work in sustainable fashion
only now I am back in that bottomless hole
of a vortex so black it has swallowed my soul
how many times can my heart yet be broken
how many times must I say my goodbyes
how many times do I wish I had spoken
language of magic but my mouth just went dry
to love and respect seemed so easy for me

to watch it now vanish I was unfit to see
I sent her on trails that were too steep for me
to expand our vision for a purpose to be
how many times can I learn to survive
how many times dare I celebrate life
how many friends wish to learn from my pain
and climb up together to live once again
I wandered the forest in ultimate sorrow,
and came out to embrace another tomorrow.
The spirit I was seeking turned up all around,
It is living inside every creature I found.

I dedicate this poem to the memory of my mother, who went into the forest she loved, where she had rested for fifty days. The earth was her pillow the stars were her blanket and the Angel who had brought her into our lives guided her home when she was ready to go. He knew the way.

In our hearts she lives on. With our hearts we can reach her. Her Spirit is everywhere.

CHAPTER TWENTY-NINE

RECOVERY

I was ill prepared to feel what I was feeling now. I was completely at wit's end. This was another big T. I had learned such coping skills as trauma will require of its victims. To be retraumatized is not the way out. New trauma gives new challenges. Coping skills are key. I was hungry for more. I had only just begun to learn. Going back to the skill acquisition:

The accident had put an end to my life as I had known it. Yet, as the crash took place, I was surrounded by people who knew me, cared for both my daughter and me. I felt lucky and grateful in my heart. Luck is a strange thing. It is not something that fell on me like morning dew. I was born on a Sunday. That made superstitious people tell me that I am lucky. They believe it. Now I must learn to feel lucky. That requires to be prepared for noticing the feeling of luck and to be patient when that feeling is not there. Now I must believe in luck too. Here it was:

Once again, I was in the company and care of a helpful friend. My doctor had referred me to the counselor who treats trauma patients without drugs as I had demanded. He has Wounded Warrior expertise. I began seeing him twice a week after his evaluation of my condition:

"You have a classic case of Post-Traumatic Stress Disorder", he said. "I am a Vietnam Veteran, injured and traumatized, healed and now it is my work, to help trauma victims. The thousands of veterans in this country (more than casualties in combat by a factor of ten) who have lost their lives by their own hands with their own weapons give testimony to a crisis of PTSD in this country. Your case is related to this, because you are the son and grandson of traumatized veterans from WW1 and WW2. You were born into trauma and raised with trauma.

You grew up surrounded by people suffering from PTSD and those with "inherited benefits."

You have suffered big trauma several times in Your life starting at age three with a third-degree burn.

You also have suffered a number of little trauma events, we call little Ts, plus you have what we call "inherited benefits", which is what happens to people who are raised by parents with PTSD.

All of these trauma events have now been reactivated. We will work on healing this trauma as the episodes reveal themselves using a method called Emotional Freedom Technique (EFT) which is done with the use of tapping on certain meridian points of the body, while reciting issues of concern, beginning with a statement of self-love and self -acceptance.

Issues such as injuries, pain, worries, hurts of any kind, relationship issues, work related issues, anything at all that concerns, hurts or worries you can be addressed in this way. It can be done anytime day or night in response to whatever comes up. You can keep a written list of issues, big ones on top and smaller ones towards the end. Rewrite the list once in a while. See what happens to these issues of concern. Issues have a way of resolving themselves and to disappear.

At the same time, we will be working on developing coping skills.

The mantra we use in EFT is:

"I love, honor and accept myself just the way I am, even though ……

Then we speak the first issue on top of the list, for example:

"I have almost lost my life in a head on collision but I cannot forgive myself for driving my child into this accident."

This is repeated until all meridian points have been tapped eight times each.

Beginning at the outside of the palm (right or left) and continuing from the top of the head to the eyebrow, the outside of the eye, under the nose, the front of the chin, the collarbone, under the arm and down to the outside of the hand between little and ring fingers.

For a time, we did these tapping sessions together, until I was finding my routine of going from pressure point to pressure point, reciting one item from the top of my list of over two hundred issues and concerns.

This technique was introduced by Gary Craig and is now widely used to treat PTSD and other anxiety disorders. Benefits include lowering the heart rate of patients and increasing the oxygen level of the blood. (see Google Emotional Freedom Technique)

The second mantra we use is the Polynesian OponoPono Prayer of people in Hawaii:

We used it by repeating it eight times, addressing a person who could be anywhere on the planet. We use water to be the conductor of this message. It is a heart to heart contact that is beneficial for both the sender and the recipient. It eases burdens that can crush people.

I am sorry.
Please forgive me.
I thank You.
I love You.

"This is a powerful prayer, that causes the burden of knowing about challenges or injuries to be shared and thereby making them easier to bear." My trauma coach said.

We went to work while the world kept on caving in around me.

I was lucky and blessed by my friends and family who did not hesitate to hold me up when I was falling and to support me the best they could.

I was lucky that I had music in my background and in my inner ear I was able to run classical music from memory that could create harmony at will.

My car stereo was also permanently set on a classical channel.

Most importantly I was able to return to the Island where my injured knees were not exposed to the ice and snow events of Maine winters. Luckily, I was now surrounded by my community of the last forty Years and found generous support at every turn. I was able to continue therapy including personal training and workouts in the water at the Pool. I found a very talented yoga teacher for restorative stretch. My trauma treatment was continuing with new variations and new challenges such as my divorce negotiations and endless insurance issues and medical challenges that did require legal help and finding new solutions for building the mental steps to get back to the light.

I am falling.
Dying seems easier than living.

A little voice inside says:
Forgive yourself.
Love yourself.
How can I?
I ask.
Try.

I began to climb one little step at a time. I spent a lot of time in the slow lane of the pool where I could not fall down. I was setting small achievable goals for myself. In the winter I was living on Island. I walked into a restaurant. It turned out to be an art space for the Winter, promoting writing, poetry, crafts, painting, music and art fusion projects. It inspired me to do an improvisation (it started with my writing my name into the presenters list, thinking it was the guest list.) There I was, on the open mike giving a narrative. It reaffirmed my desire to write. I was trying to get tall again after being bent over for some Years, from a protective stance, favoring my ribcage, arms and knees. Now I wanted to straighten up and get tall. Tango came to mind. I joined a ballroom dancing group. It was very hard. I tangoed for one session. Goal reached. I was on to something. In a film I heard a dancer explain Tango. She said:

"Tango is a shared language. It is trust, discipline, rhythm, attention, intuition, sensation, desire. There are no lies. There is just the dance. Steps taken together, no leader, no follower. Both pay attention and sense the partner's moves."

Tango was the lift I was reaching for.

I spoke to the creator of this art Space about my hope to find a Tango partner to do a performance piece after reading a script followed by a dance. She asked me about my reasons and I explained about my accident and my recovery and about my discovery that Tango might give me another lift. I explained my vision of creating a performance piece with narrative.

It would involve learning the language of Tango and writing the story of my accident which I would read followed by acting to music the lifting up the victim and a person appearing at that moment, noticing the music and the reaction of the fallen person, lifting him with attention, beginning movement, a transformation to dance ending in a short Tango.

I received a letter in the mail sometime after this interview, with an honorarium, which I spent taking Tango lessons in Germany at a Tango loft.

Together with her terrific team, my sponsor encouraged me to write about my journey and history and to take a creative leap into performing a Tango.

This project helped me get through the heartbreak of losing my family.

I was unprepared. I had no idea how to cope. The bond between me and my child's mother tore apart. In my injured state I was no longer able to live with other people in the same space. Without thinking, I began collecting outdoor survival gear, so I would be prepared to disappear somewhere outside, like all the other homeless victims of PTSD.

I began to discover the role music was playing in my life. I now found myself escaping into the refuge of this vast world of music that I was able to play back in my mind whenever I needed to get away. The other place that was therapeutic and nurturing for me was the water of the pool in which I did physical therapy.

Helpful in addition to the beneficial effect of water, was my growing meditation skill, that I was able to bring along to do water meditation focused on gratitude and forgiveness. The third place that revived my broken heart was a mountain made of ancient granite overgrown with moss, grass and a variety of pine, fir, hemlock, birch, poplar, ash and oak. Vegetation creates an ever-changing pallet of colors and textures. Walking in this wilderness was un-estimable because in my life growing up, the outdoors was the safe place for me. Here I found elements that helped me reach a place from which I could see the light. To survive, I was using positive energy. I was aided by my trauma coach. EFT was helping in a consistent way. I was now beginning to grieve for my lost life, a loss that no one else can see or feel. A loss for which there are no words and ending life is a real temptation, it is the easy way out. Grieving on the other hand was a positive force for me.

In the Summer of 2012, I had a list of one hundred and twelve Items I was worried about, hurt by, or unsure what to do about. In the Summer of 2013, I was down to four. In the Fall of 2014, I was down to none. Some physical impairments are not repairable, but manageable.

The method I used to stay on track was to set tiny achievable goals. Qualify for the next step in recovery. Expect inevitable setbacks. Triggers still exist and often do not announce themselves. They can cause my heart to run at two hundred and twenty beats per minute. Sudden sensation of pitch-black despair happens out of the blue. Inability to see the light, or a way out, new injuries caused by malfunctions in the brain. Knee jerks causing new outrageous pain that would take weeks to heal, all were now stepping stones on the way up.

My life had provided me with injuries that gave me a very high tolerance for pain, no bad mood from pain, no surprises, no anger. Protecting my body had bent me over. I decided to do something constructive in that posture. I set a twelve-month goal to enable myself to harvest grapes. I went to work at the pool, building upper body strength and stamina. After succeeding with the task of harvesting grapes in 2012, I celebrated by setting the next goal: To become tall again and walk like a human. For this I needed Yoga, Music and Dance. The method for achieving this, was Ballroom dancing, with the objective to Tango during the winter of 2012/2013, even if it was just one Tango. I had come out of the hole; my life skills were returning one at a time. Tango was going to lift me up and straighten my posture.

Music was another force that gave me the incentive to dare life, rather than to succumb to the easy way to simply quit and die.

Skiing: The quest for snow was not new to me. I had access to more hand-me down skis as a young boy than to snow. The bindings were those bone breakers you see on skis mounted crosswise to walls of ski lodges.

Now the next step for me was to get back onto skis. I booked a package with rental of demos and lodging plus a perfect turn clinic. I repeated this for a couple of years and have found my comfort zone on groomed snow. I cried from joy after the first run and I was very moved when the instructor told me that the only way for me to get better at perfect turns was to teach the class myself. I practiced all the moves in the water of the pool.

Sailing: It is the shortest way to get as far away from every-day life, as one can, it takes all of my attention and all my senses to notice the vessel, the wind, the temperature the commands of the captain and the movements of the teammates, to be in tune with every maneuver, that has to be performed in perfect coordination with everyone on board. Then you have a chance to place or to win. My position on the boat was the "Pit". Raise and lower sails. Have the Lines and Halyards in order and ready to go in a split second. Come up, sit on the high rail, cross over in turns. Be ready for sail changes. Even though I was unable to scramble across the deck with my injured knees, the team was very generous to let me participate in a race week in June of 2009. I was desperately trying to get my life back. At this point I did not even know all the injuries I had suffered. My chest was broken and my knees did not obey. I stayed below and helped to balance the boat by tucking myself as close to the underside of the rail as I could. We took third place and I was very moved when my teammates and my skipper gave me the trophy at the end of the season. I had to retire from sailing. I was much more broken than I had imagined. I took many very dear memories with me from my sailing adventures, from towing the first boat across the country around the clock, three tank fills on, two tank fills off, until we had the boat safely at the east coast. Then first regattas when the teammates asked where the best place for sunbathing would be and how soon beer and food was going to be served and where is the bathroom? From here we went all the way to a well-trained, very motivated team that was bringing trophies home on a regular basis showing first, second and third place finishes regularly. One trip was an overnight cruise from City Island to the Cape, when the fog set in and with steady wind from the west I spent the night in the forward basket. Having only fifty feet visibility. Outside of Newport we avoided crashing into a huge steel wall that came out of the fog white on white in dim light. We were able to head into the wind and thereby avoided sinking the Q. E. 2 with our 34-foot boat. I will never forget the joy of seeing the final lighthouse.

With gratitude I wish to express my love and admiration for my daughter who was in the car with me when all this started and who is the rock that is there when I reach for it. She was instrumental in the completion of this memoir and a novel that spun off of it during the process. I dedicate this memoir to her.

November 2019

Printed in the United States
By Bookmasters